Group Games
Dealing with Aggression

Other Titles in the Group Games Series

Group Games
Dealing with Aggression

ROSEMARIE PORTMANN

Speechmark

Speechmark Publishing Ltd
Telford Road • Bicester • Oxon OX26 4LQ • United Kingdom

Originally published in German by Don Bosco Verlag München under the title *Spiele zum Umgang mit Aggressionen* © Don Bosco Verlag, München 1998

Published by
Speechmark Publishing Ltd, Telford Road, Bicester, Oxon OX26 4LQ, UK
www.speechmark.net

© Speechmark Publishing Ltd, 2002

Reprinted 2003

002-5124/Printed in the United Kingdom/1010

British Library Cataloguing in Publication Data

Portmann, Rosemarie
   Dealing with aggression. – (Group Games)
   1. Aggressiveness in children 2. Group games
   I. Title
   155.4'182'32

ISBN 0 86388 410 5

Contents

About the Author

Rosemarie Portmann Dip (Psychol) is the manager of the educational psychology service for the local education authority in Wiesbaden, Germany. She is also an adviser to the Parents Association in Hessen.

Rosemarie is a lecturer at the Institute for Educational Pedagogy and Teaching Methods in the Elementary and Primary Department of the University of Frankfurt.

She is the author of several successful games books and other specialist publications, including *Emotional Strength & Self-Esteem,* and co-author of *Relaxation & Concentration*, both in Speechmark's *Group Games* series.

Acknowledgement

Thank you to Lilo Seelos, the translator.

Note: The text sometimes refers to the leader or the child as 'he', for the sake of clarity alone.

Games

Building Up Inner Strength & Self-Esteem — 131

Building Non-Aggressive Relationships — 151

Resolving Conflicts Peacefully

Introduction

**LEARNING TO LIVE PEACEFULLY WITH ANGER
AND AGGRESSION**
Children, teenagers and adults today have a reputation for being extremely self-centred and increasingly aggressive. Their opportunities for social experiences have decreased owing to changes in the conditions for socialisation; families becoming smaller, and human relationships becoming more fragile. Many find it difficult to build up positive contacts with others; to integrate themselves into a group; to give time and attention to each other; to hold back, and to resolve conflicts constructively.

In fact, complaints about aggressiveness in children and teenagers, and the difficulty of dealing with them, are not as new as many case studies would like to make out. Aggressive behaviour in children and teenagers has been described as most disturbing and difficult to influence for many years. It is therefore all the more surprising that educational efforts to develop counter-methods and measures have done nothing to address these continuing complaints. Educational possibilities are frequently not utilised. The education of feelings often plays no part. Skills that children and teenagers have to acquire to help them control their angry and aggressive impulses, and to develop and maintain satisfying relationships with others, are not practised. The skills and willingness to practise constructive, peaceful conflict resolution behaviour are rarely taught.

Mostly, children and teenagers are simply urged to 'get on with each other'. Educational methods are strongly based on harmonisation, which is more about the prevention of conflicts than about seriously getting involved in problems. Conflicts are predominantly dealt with in a conventional way, by trying to find and reprimand the person 'at fault'. The social environment reacts to aggressive behaviour with punishment, retaliation, and social rejection. This is perceived by the person concerned as an additional threat, and does not lead to a decrease in their anger and aggression, but instead creates new aggressions.

In addition, the term 'aggression' carries some ambivalence in modern society. In many cases, aggression is rewarded: people need to approach life with a healthy portion of aggression and fighting spirit. Every sports reporter demands more aggressiveness from football players when they look like losing. It is not without reason that uncontrolled, physically harmful arguments are predominantly a problem of boys and male teenagers.

The conscious, focused handling of anger and aggression is necessary. This is not just a matter of making children and teenagers 'give up' anger, aggression and arguing.

Anger is a tense inner state of irritation that will always recur, and must not just be 'swallowed'. A person who keeps their feelings in check loses their liveliness, and does not give those around them a chance to react. Aggressiveness is not always the same as violence. Even though the term is generally equated with deliberate destruction, or the cause of physical or psychological pain, the word 'aggression' actually means 'self-assertive', 'forceful', and describes power, both positive and negative. If we want to get along with others, we need to learn how to argue. Uninterrupted harmony would make life boring and unbearable. Different opinions and interests make it attractive: they have to be expressed; conflicts have to be resolved – without mutual injury and damage. For this, people of all ages need support.

HOW GROUP GAMES AND ACTIVITIES CAN HELP

Group games and activities are an easy-to-learn and cheap means of kick-starting educational processes for the constructive management of anger and aggression. Games offer children and teenagers open systems for interaction that enable them to have diverse experiences with themselves as well as others. They can bring their feelings and needs into the game situation; participate actively and with self-determination, and experience the consequences of their actions without any fear.

This is particularly true of social games: that is, exercises and games without victory and defeat. Competitive games do not lend themselves to promoting positive social processes. Wanting to win leads to strong psychological tension, so that different, socially desirable, behaviour patterns cannot be learned. Social games and activities, however, facilitate varied relationships between group members, not only at a factual, but also at an emotional level. During social games, children and teenagers can overcome routine behaviour patterns, and practise skills that are necessary for positive social behaviour.

Playing stimulates important learning processes, yet playing is not a 'serious' situation. Many things that might be embarrassing, or carry sanctions, are allowed in games, and can bring fun. Associated with this are, for example, the following:

- The dynamics of tension and relaxation
- The releasing of imagination, including nonsense with some games, for example, word games
- Movement and body contact in many games
- Permitted 'aggressive' behaviour
- The enjoyment that comes from recognition, safety and increased fun through repetition.

During social games, interactions are experienced particularly clearly, because they are ritualised through the rules of the game. These interactive rituals serve a number of different functions:

- The socially controlled structuring of everyday situations
- The selective reduction of complexity, because they promote interaction by reducing different behaviour
- Through this, they reduce uncertainty and fear.

During social games, aggressive behaviour can be utilised strategically through selection and rule-based rituals and, thus, can be turned into useful non-aggressive intentions. In addition, games and other activities can help to let off a certain amount of steam, and thus serve to reduce tension. Playing in a group creates a basis for having conversations about a topic, as everyone starts from the same or similar experiences (as they have previously shared experiences). This has a different quality from a lecture, a piece of text, or a film as an introduction.

Children and teenagers who behave aggressively often have disturbed body awareness. They are unable to accept 'positive' body contacts. During play, especially during movement games, they can learn to explore and rule their own bodies, to be touched and to touch others in a friendly way. Movement games are particularly important in connection with anger and aggression, because often the psycho-motor needs of children and teenagers are not considered enough.

During group activities and games, aggression can be ritualised. Such aggression rituals ('pretend fights') have a number of benefits:

◆ They serve to help express anger and hostility
◆ They permit an eased regression; that is, they lead away from societal constraints
◆ Reciprocal, irrational attacks within a ritual framework create solidarity and trust among those involved

◆ They make participants more aware of the way society defines aggressive behaviour
◆ Taboos, such as swear words, can be used without embarrassment or sanctions
◆ Role reversals, including hierarchical reversals, are possible.

Aggression rituals are not just a matter of 'playing about'; they are common practice in many different societies. However, rituals, as expressed during group activities and games, also hide a danger – that of serving an apparently liberating function without being really liberating. This is one reason why subsequent discussion of participants' experiences during the game is important.

While the possibilities of social games have not been exhausted by a long way, they should not be overvalued. Games and activities can help to balance social learning deficits, and to provide social and emotional experiences. Through variations, they can be geared to the needs and situations of a particular group. However, they are not a general cure, and under no circumstances are they therapy!

For uncommunicative people of all ages games and activities often facilitate access to their emotions more than conversations. The more positive play experiences they can have, the more likely they are to open up. Of course, this will only succeed if the games and activities take place in a pleasant atmosphere; if younger participants in particular are treated with respect, and their needs are taken seriously.

Group games and activities can be the basis of specific learning goals, such as:

◆ Perceiving and expressing aggressive feelings
◆ Recognising triggers for anger and aggression
◆ Understanding oneself and others better
◆ Controlling and reducing anger and aggression
◆ Building inner strength and self-esteem
◆ Building non-aggressive relationships
◆ Resolving conflicts peacefully.

Specific goals cannot always be clearly separated. The categorisation of games and activities according to learning goals is made more difficult because of their complexity, which may not resemble real events. It is only possible to set main focuses. The categorisation of the group games within this book under the above learning goals should be viewed with this limitation in mind.

Notes on the Activities
This book contains activities and games that have been tested in practice. During the selection, care was taken to ensure that as many different opportunities as possible were presented for holistic learning.

Age ranges for players and possibilities for variations have been omitted deliberately. Most activities and games can be carried out with people of different ages without any problems, as long as content and rules are adapted accordingly. To ensure that games and exercises facilitate the intended learning processes, they have to be adapted sensitively to the actual status of the group and its individual members.

These games and activities generally do not require any special preparation. The large majority can be carried out without any materials. Any everyday materials that may be needed are listed at the beginning of the game.

One precondition for the success of these games and activities is the endeavour to create a trusting climate within the group. Despite this, you may find that individuals do not want to participate. They must not be forced to participate, but should remain in the room. Not all people fell able to get involved with others – which is, of course, one of the aims of the games. However, they can gradually gain trust through unpressurised observation, and become closer to what is happening in the game – until, in the end, they participate. On the whole, disturbances caused by very insecure children and teenagers stop after an initial period of getting used to the games. Experience has shown that, in the end, the games and activities are enjoyed by everybody.

After every activity, there should be time for follow-up work and evaluation. Allow people the opportunity to talk about their experiences and feelings during the activities, or to express them through words, pictures, movements or scenic representations.

Group leaders do not require special qualifications to use these activities. However, they should themselves enjoy playing, and should try out every game and every exercise themselves – ideally with others – before offering them to a group.

Games &
Exercises for
Dealing with
Aggression

Perceiving & Expressing Aggressive Feelings

It has been claimed that not only are children and teenagers in particular behaving in an increasingly aggressive manner, but that this aggressive behaviour is becoming more and more inconsiderate and unrestrained. They continue to torture and abuse their victims, even when the latter have already been defeated or seriously hurt. They overstep boundaries, because they have no awareness of the feelings of others.

Socially aggressive children and teenagers also often have no access to their own feelings. In order to be able to differentiate and consciously perceive the feelings of others, they first have to learn to become conscious of their own feelings; to accept them, and to express them clearly and unambiguously. Children and teenagers have to be able to experience the fact that anger, rage and aggression are feelings that belong to every human being and therefore it is alright to have these feelings, and to express them without becoming scared or having to feel guilty. Anger, rage and aggression, then, can only be controlled and managed constructively if they no longer have to be suppressed. In the process, creative exercises and games can open up new possibilities of expression and coping. How people deal with their own feelings, and those of others, is a decisive criterion for the way they live together and get along with each other.

1 When I am Angry

The group is seated in a circle. One after the other, everyone says their name and demonstrates what they do when they are angry. For example:

'My name is Rosemary. When I am angry, I do this'. (makes a movement with her hand as if she is going to hit someone)

'My name is Thomas. When I am angry, I do this'. (makes a movement with his foot as if he is going to kick someone)

'My name is John. When I am angry, I do this'. (drums with both fists against his temples)

And so on.

The game can also serve as a getting-to-know-each-other game, and as an introduction to the treatment of 'anger' and 'aggression'. It becomes more difficult if it is played as a 'round' game: every one has to repeat all the names and expressions of anger of the people before them, before they can add their own name and 'outburst of rage'.

2 Have You Seen Angry Tom?

Everyone is seated in a circle, except one person who walks around in the middle. Suddenly he stops in front of another person and asks: 'Have you seen angry Tom?' The person answers, 'Yes.' Then the person in the middle asks: 'What did he do?' The seated person now demonstrates what the 'angry Tom' did – an aggressive gesture, an angry noise, or both together; then everyone in the circle joins in.

After a while, the seated person stops gesturing, as does everyone else. The two now swap places and a new round begins.

Body Language

Each person is given a piece of paper on which is written details of the sort of emotion – being anxious, being very hurt, being annoyed, being angry, being affectionate, and so on – they are supposed to portray. If necessary, the same emotion can be handed out to different people. After every portrayal, the group tries to guess which emotion was being expressed.

In the end, the group works out through joint discussion how the different emotions can be identified.

Which emotions were easier to portray and to recognise than others? Which emotions are expressed in a similar way, so that we have to pay close attention to recognise them?

4 **Painting Feelings**

For this exercise, paper and coloured pens or water colours are needed.

The group members paint the feelings they have when they are 'losing it': rage, anger, fear, omnipotence – depending on personality, situation and mood. Anyone who wants to can then explain their picture; the personal connection to the emotions portrayed should become clear.

In a second round of painting, group members can experiment to discover how their emotions picture can be influenced positively through over painting, adding different colours or shapes, and so on, so that, for example, 'aggression' can turn into 'friendship', and 'fear' can turn into 'self-confidence'. How easy or difficult do individuals find it to paint their emotions? How easy or difficult is it to turn anger into calm?

5 Symbols of Aggression

The group are seated at a table. Everyone has a large piece of paper in front of them, and a pen. When everyone has settled down, they draw a symbol for their very personal kind of aggression on the paper. Afterwards, each person writes a brief explanation about their symbol of aggression. For example:

'Jagged red flashes, because my anger always comes fast and strong and disappears again equally fast.'

'Mountains and dark clouds on the horizon, because my anger tends to build up and puts me in a bad mood for quite a while, without anybody noticing that I am angry.'

'A ball of fire, because my anger is violent and destructive.'

And so on.

People can stop and close their eyes while they are painting, so they can concentrate better on their inner feelings.

When everyone has finished, time should be given to compare and discuss the different symbols in the group. At the end, all symbols can be collected on a poster and put up somewhere in the room. Frequent examination of the poster can contribute to the understanding of one's own and other people's symbols of aggression.

(6) Sharing the Anger

Group members who do not get along with each other too well, and easily get into arguments paint an 'anger picture'. They sit down opposite each other with a piece of paper between them and take it in turns – without talking to each other – line by line, to draw on the paper. While they are doing this they try to examine the feelings they harbour for each other. Sometimes, just the joint activity helps them to get closer to each other.

An opportunity should be given afterwards to talk to each other in a small group or as a whole group. What did they feel while they were drawing together with a person whom they disliked?

7   A Picture of Aggression

Every group member cuts out a picture from an old magazine or newspaper that, in their view, expresses the emotion 'aggression'. Afterwards, pictures are looked at together. The group selects some of the pictures and discusses these together. If the group is not too big, all of the pictures should be talked about.

Are there contents, colours, shapes, forms of expression and so on that were selected particularly often – that were especially easily associated with 'aggression'? Are there people who chose very similar, or maybe even the same pictures?

8 With Mixed Emotions

A randomly chosen sentence is spoken while expressing should be said with different feelings: for example, 'Children should go to school every day.' To do this, group members each draw a card on which a word representing a particular emotion is written: eg, angry, friendly, sad, arrogant, curious. Then they have to try to express the chosen sentence in that way, using tone of voice, mime and gesture. The rest of the group try to guess the particular emotion.

How well did the group members express their emotion? How difficult was it to portray particular emotions using voice and those gestures that are possible while sitting? Which means of expression did people use? Did the sentence take on a different meaning according to the emotion portrayed?

9) Collected Anger

Group members collect 'anger words' by approaching others and requesting a word. Those who are being approached must think of a word, write it on a card or piece of paper, and hand it over.

Once all group members have collected between five and 10 different words in this way, they use them – in combination with any filler words – in an 'anger poem' or an 'anger story'. It is also acceptable for poet pairs or poet groups to get together. For example, if the collected words were 'cross', 'punch-up', 'fight', 'kick', 'telling tales' and 'idiot', the anger poem could sound like this:

> After the fight on the hills
> I am going to have a punch-up with Henry.
> First a push and then a kick!
> I am cross, cross, cross!
> That idiot always has to tell tales,
> stirring up people against me ...

The completed anger poems are read out loud and, possibly complete with pictures, put up in the group room or put together as an 'anger book'.

10 ABC of Swear-words

Generally, people do not like to hear swear-words. However, swearing can be extremely liberating. That is why, in this exercise, everyone is allowed to swear to their heart's content.

Every person writes down the letters of the alphabet one under the other (x, y and z may be left out), and finds as many swear-words or pejorative terms beginning with each letter as possible. 'Taboo words' should be allowed, too.

Of course, the group can also come up with a joint swear-word ABC. Does everybody actually know what the swear-words mean? Which words are particularly hurtful? Why?

11 Pointless Rage

Group members are asked to invent short words that, in their opinion, express anger and aggression, for example: 'zap', 'zing', 'zonk', 'kapow', and so on. Afterwards, they try to work out together why they have come up with precisely *these* meaningless words.

Are there particular characteristics of an 'aggression and anger' word? Are there sounds that can be used to express anger particularly well?

Maybe the group's preferred swear-words and curses could, in future, be replaced by such meaningless 'anger words'? Some conflict situations can be defused, and the same old 'aggression circles' can be broken up in this way.

12 Chain of Fury

Building word chains is a popular game. For an 'anger word chain', group members are best seated in a circle. One begins with an 'anger word', the next links up with another that begins with the last letter of the first word, and so on. For example:

anger — rage — envious — sucker — rotter — rat

How many 'anger words' can the group think of? Which words are given preference?

13 Anger Chain Reaction

The first person names a particular situation that makes them angry. The second reacts with a swear-word or anything else 'angry' that they can think of, and then names an anger-triggering situation themselves, to which the third person again reacts with an 'anger word', and so on. For example:

Person 1: homework

Person 2: damn waste of time
fighting with Petra

Person 3: silly cow
not being allowed out

Person 4: …

What sort of situations and reactions are named? Are they real situations for the group members? How do the children deal with them in reality?

(14) Talking Big

The group members walk around the room, and act out angry and aggressive phrases that are called out by the group leader. For example:

◆ Chopping off someone's head
◆ Pulling your hair out
◆ Red rag to a bull
◆ Feeling crabby
◆ Being in a black mood
◆ Making someone's blood boil
◆ Picking a bone with someone
◆ Having a short temper
◆ Hopping mad

Afterwards, the group discusses what these sayings actually mean; how they came about, and whether they are still appropriate today. Are there other possibilities for expressing one's own anger?

15 Being Scared – Scaring Others

There are not only common sayings for anger, but also for fear. On two wall posters, the group can collect synonyms, descriptions and sayings for both types of behaviour:

◆ *Being scared*: holding one's breath, cold sweat, going pale, wanting the ground to open up, going quiet, and so on;
◆ *Scaring others:* raging, red with anger, doing someone in, cold-blooded, losing one's temper, and so on.

Afterwards, the group can talk about whether there are links between the two and, if so, what they are.

Are those people who scare others sometimes scared themselves? What of?

16 Loud Post

The group remains seated wherever they happen to be, or they form a circle. One of them begins by shouting an 'anger word' at the next person: for example, 'Damn you!', 'Idiot', or something similar. That person passes on the word as quickly as possible by shouting it, and the game continues thus so that, in the end, all participants have been shouted at once and have shouted once themselves, until the 'anger word' has returned to the original sender, the first person. Then the next round can begin with a new word, and so on, until the group has shouted itself out.

During the course of the game, the sender can change the direction, to bring even more tension into the game. The 'anger words' can also refer to a current occasion. The exercise can help to reduce initial anger in a ritualised way during a difficult group situation.

(17) Hopping Mad

The following exercise can be useful to express and, at the same time, reduce a tense group atmosphere.

Group members turn into wild animals. For example, they snarl and stalk about the room like tigers, crawl and hiss like snakes, stamp about and trumpet like elephants, walk and howl like wolves. They threaten each other, but are not allowed to really attack the other animals: they must stick to making threatening gestures, because, you never know, the other animal might be stronger and more dangerous.

After a while, everyone gathers for a peaceful 'animal conference'.

18 Journey to the Land of Fury

A leader tells a story with movement instructions, and the group join in making the movements and possibly inventing some additional ones:

Today, we are going on a long journey to a mystery country. We have to be on a train for a long, long time. [The group members join up in a long line and move around the room making train noises.] The train stops. We are in the country of joy. People who live here are always happy and jolly. They are already happy when they wake up in the morning. They have a good stretch, greet us with laughter, jump about, hug us and dance with us, in pairs, in threesomes, in a large circle. No one is left out … Unfortunately, we can't stop. We have to carry on. I can hear the train's whistle. We get in and travel on and on … All of a sudden it becomes dark. The train stops. We are in the land of fury. The people who live here feel hurt and ill-treated. They are angry and furious, stamp their feet, throw themselves to the floor, pull their hair, shake their heads, clench their fists, shout: 'I hate you' … Finally, the train calls us back. We stop, take a deep breath … and become calm again. We get in and continue our journey … Our train stops: the final stop. We are in the land of calm, everyone here smiles, moves about calmly and carefully, they stroke each other, lead each other by the hand, or sit still and peacefully together …

There are no boundaries to the imagination during the journey. Some countries can be so far away, or so difficult to get to, that 'travellers' may need to get on a ship, an aeroplane or even a space rocket. In any case, the journey should end in a land of calm and harmony.

How did the group feel during the journey? How are they feeling now the journey is over?

(19) What Annoys Me About You ...

This exercise gives every group member the chance to give someone else a piece of their mind. Every complaint is introduced with: 'You are actually very nice, but what annoys me about you ...'. The person being addressed is not allowed to justify themselves, but, instead, has to answer: 'Thank you for telling me.' This exercise works best with the group sitting in a circle. One person summons up the courage to begin. They stand up and walk over to the person who they are going to speak to. For example: 'Sue, you are actually very nice, but what annoys me about you is that you always want to play with Julia, and she is *my* friend.' Sue answers: 'Thank you for telling me.' Then it is the next person's turn, and so on until everyone who wants to have a go has voiced their annoyance about another person. Only then are the group members given an opportunity to talk about their feelings and experiences during the exercise. What did it feel like when you had to start by saying something friendly to a person who annoys you? What does it feel like to be attacked without being allowed to fight back? How are the people feeling who did not 'have a go' at anybody?

This exercise presupposes a basic trust within the group, and should be utilised with extra care.

Recognising Triggers for Anger & Aggression

Anger and aggression, in others as well as in oneself, do not simply come out of the blue. They do not just happen to us unexpectedly. Behaviour and actions are always determined by concrete motives. Anger, rage and aggression in children, adolescents and adults often develop when their needs have not been satisfied, or their expectations and goals have not been achieved. In such situations, they may take out their anger on totally uninvolved people or objects if they are unable to focus it on the cause of their aggression, because that person may be too powerful or simply not available. Among the basic needs of children and adolescents are the need to be worth something; the need to be able to do things; the need to be socially accepted, and the need to belong. The desire to gain intrinsic value through superiority in a social hierarchy – that is the wish to be bigger, better, faster, more attractive than others just for once, is a classical trigger of aggressive confrontations.

In the end, anger and aggression do not involve 'bad intention against others'; rather they are an (inappropriate) attempt to 'do oneself some good'.

Knowing the motives for anger and aggression still does not necessarily mean we have a handle on aggressive behaviour, but it does mean that we can deal with it more easily. If we want to positively influence socially aggressive children and adolescents, we have to open up possibilities for them to satisfy their justified needs and assert their interests.

20 Excluded

The group walk around the room and play 'greetings scenarios': they shake hands, smile at each other, exchange a few words, say goodbyes, carry on walking, greet the next person that they meet, and so on.

Only one person is ignored. He has volunteered to take on the role of the person who is excluded. He now has to try to be included in the group again. The game ends when he has succeeded in shaking another person's hand, or struck up a conversation with them.

How difficult was it for the excluded person to break through the rejection of the others? What did being excluded and trying to be included again feel like? How did the others feel when they were not allowed to include that particular person?

21 What Have They Done to You?

One person is chosen to be the culprit. While the others are freely walking around the room, the culprit finds a victim to whom he whispers a swear-word in passing, or whom he touches without anyone else noticing. Hitting, pinching, or other painful touching, is not allowed.

The victim stops and begins to complain and whimper. The others now try to guess what has been done to the victim. If they succeed, the victim becomes quiet again and everyone continues their walk. The person who guessed correctly first becomes the new culprit and is allowed to find a new victim. The game becomes easier if either just touching or just swearing is permitted, and if possible touches or swear-words should be discussed before the game begins.

22 The Evil Eye

The group is seated in a circle. Prior to the start of play, it is decided who is going to have the 'evil eye' by having a secret drawing of lots – only the person concerned is in the know as to who has the 'evil eye'.

This person now begins to catch others by staring, winking and so on at them. Any one who feels 'caught' says, 'I've been hit', and moves away from the circle without having their 'hit' confirmed by the person with the 'evil eye'. Everyone in the circle watches carefully what is going on, and tries to find out who has the 'evil eye'. If someone who has not yet been hit thinks they may have identified the person, they raise their hand and call out, 'I am applying for an arrest warrant for …'. The game continues until the person with the 'evil eye' has been found out.

The game is not as easy as it sounds: people will feel caught even when they are not being aimed at, or not even being looked at; 'innocent' people will be suspected of having the 'evil eye'.

A discussion afterwards can focus on the ease with which human perception and judgement can cause rumours and character assassination on the one hand, and paranoia on the other hand.

23 Make Way!

Everyone walks around the room with firm steps. Using their elbows, they pretend to make room for themselves – without actually touching anybody – and, at the same time, shout: 'Make way, I am coming through!'

At the leader's shout, the group gradually increase their walking pace, and the shouting also gets increasingly louder – until everybody abruptly stops, again at the the leader's shout. Everyone freezes in the position that they were in at the time.

At a new signal, everyone finds a space and a position in which they feel comfortable and are not in anyone's way. From there they begin, again at the leader's call, to amble leisurely around the room and greet anybody they meet with a friendly smile. This exercise works best when it is supported by corresponding mime.

After the exercise, there is an opportunity for discussion. How did participants feel during the different phases of the game? How do they feel anyway as part of the group? Do they have enough 'space' for themselves? Do they feel too restricted or too 'boundless'? What would other group members have to do so they can be within the group and feel comfortable?

(**24**) Listen to My Command

Everyone likes to be the centre of attention. A simple game can provide an opportunity for this. The group sit or stand in a circle; one person stands in the middle and demonstrates movements and noises that everyone else has to copy. They can change the movement as often as they want.

Sometimes, when playing this game, the group will see a previously unnoticed person in a new light – maybe he is more imaginative, more agile, funnier than the others had thought or perceived him to be? The person in the middle either has a set time to give commands, or he changes roles with someone who has copied him particularly well.

25　Who is in Charge Here?

One person is sent outside the room. The others are seated or stand in a circle, and decide who is in charge. This person begins with a movement that he keeps changing as quickly and seamlessly as possible. Everyone else must watch inconspicuously, and copy the movement and any changes. The person outside is called in and stands in the middle of the circle, and tries to find out who is controlling the movement of the group.

Was it easy for the group to follow the leader inconspicuously? Was it difficult to control the group inconspicuously, but in a determined manner?

26 Scaling the Wall

Three to four people at a time form a human 'wall', and another person then tries to get through or over the wall. Physical attacks that hurt or injure are not allowed. After the wall has been breached, or after an agreed period of time, roles are reversed so that every person who wants to is given the opportunity to attack the wall.

How often is the 'wall attack' successful? What was particularly helpful for overcoming the wall? What does one feel like as 'the wall', or as the person trying to overcome the wall? Are there some people who did not even try to get over the wall?

(27) Castle Attack

Instead of a wall (see 'Scaling the Wall' on the previous page), the group can create a 'castle' – that is a firmly closed circle – which one person tries to break into from the outside, or tries to get out of from the inside. For this castle attack, the group can also subdivide into two smaller groups, for example into girls and boys. First, the boys are given the task of building a castle, using their bodies. The girls try to attack the castle. Afterwards, roles are reversed: the girls build the castle, the boys try – without any violence – to attack it.

How did girls and boys, respectively, feel in the different roles? Did they act differently? If so, what explanations might there be for this? Did physical strength always give the advantage? What can people achieve together that one of them on their own may not manage?

28 Codeword

A few people leave the room. Those remaining form a tight circle, linking arms. They agree a codeword – for example 'friendship' – or a 'code action' – for example pointing to the smallest person in the circle – which will open the circle from the outside.

The people outside are called in and told that they must guess the codeword or code action. They are allowed to consult each other while doing this. If they are successful, they are immediately included in the circle.

How do the excluded people feel when it takes them a long time, or if they are unable, to find the right code? How do the people in the circle feel when they have to remain firm? Can the groups help each other during the game?

29 A Group on Its Own

This exercise needs to be preceded by a discussion about outsiders and prejudice. Each group member must be prepared to experience themselves as outsiders, and to handle carefully their own prejudices against outsiders.

Next, small groups consisting of five or six people are formed. Each group decides as quickly as possible who is going to be the outsider. The outsiders from all groups form a new group.

The people in this outsider group must think about why it was they who were excluded. At the same time, the other groups must try to work out why they excluded their respective members. Afterwards, the excluded people return to their initial groups. Each group then discusses and compares the reasons, as well as the assumptions, for exclusion with each other.

Finally, the whole group focuses, first, on the feelings those who had been excluded, and then on the feelings of those who were doing the excluding. How did the conversation in the outsiders' group go? Were these people able to support each other?

This exercise should not be carried out in estranged and aggressive groups. A basic trust has to exist to ensure no one gets hurt. The leader needs empathy when putting together the smaller groups at the beginning of the exercise, and during the discussion about the feelings of individuals.

(30) This Place is Mine

The group forms a circle in the middle of which a chair is placed. One person sits on the chair and defends it against someone else, who tries for about five minutes to dispute verbally the other's right to it. Then roles are reversed.

Both sides are allowed to argue sharply, to demand, to get angry, to threaten, to insult, to beg, to flatter, to cry, and so on. *Physical attacks such as touching, pushing and kicking are not allowed.*

The scenario can also be dressed up as an everyday situation, such as the following:

◆ One person wants to take away another's book
◆ One person jealously guards the right to give out worksheets
◆ One person always wants to be first in the queue.

The game can make clear how different people present and defend their needs; how stubborn or compliant they are; how easily they can get themselves worked up over a small thing, and how helplessness, powerlessness and a lack of arguments can trigger aggression.

(**31**) Angry Like an Animal

The children are asked to imagine they are an animal: 'Which animal might you be? Now you are turning into "your" animal. You are placid and you are thinking of nothing bad. Then, suddenly, another animal turns up who you had a fight with some time ago and with whom you are still angry. What happens now? What are you doing? What is the other animal doing?'

Every child writes down (or paints) a continuation to the story. Afterwards, the stories or pictures are exhibited and discussed. The scenarios can also be role-played briefly. How quickly can a chance encounter turn into a new argument if an old one has not been resolved?

32 Excuses

People who behave aggressively towards others are often not prepared, or able, to take responsibility for their behaviour. The most common excuses for this behaviour can be uncovered with the help of this exercise.

The group members are seated in a circle. Each person is given a piece of paper and a pen. At the top of the page, they write down the beginning of a sentence that describes some sort of aggressive behaviour; for example:

◆ 'I hit him …'
◆ 'I threw the stone …'
◆ 'I called her a "stupid cow" …'.

Then they fold the paper, so the writing cannot be seen, and pass it on around the circle. The next child adds something to the sentence that begins with 'because', and includes a typical justification for an outburst of rage. For example:

◆ ' … because he tried to chat up my girl friend'
◆ ' … because it was my chair'
◆ ' … because she started it'.

They now add a new 'aggressive' sentence beginning, fold the piece of paper over, and pass it on. And so the game proceeds. When the pieces of paper are full they are unfolded and read out.

Afterwards, a discussion can highlight how often – in the exercise and in reality – certain aggressive behaviour patterns and their supposed causes repeat themselves, and how often it is more a question of bad habits than of justified outbursts of rage, and of excuses rather than causes.

33 Anger Pairs

The group divides into pairs. Each person now tries to think back to a situation when they were very angry. They think of a suitable heading for the event, and then write that heading on a piece of paper. The pieces of paper are then swapped with their partner's. The other person now has to think of an event that may be described by the heading, and write it down in a few words. For example, person 1 has written 'The missed bus'. Person 2 might write, 'John was cross because he had missed the bus. Now he was going to be late for football training and he would not be in the team for the next game.'

Afterwards, pairs discuss the results. Does the imagined event come close to the actual one? The most interesting experiences should also be discussed within the whole group.

(34) A Picture of My Anger

From a large collection of pictures, taken from magazines, catalogues, brochures, postcards and similar sources, each person chooses a picture that they associate with aggressive feelings, or that triggers aggressive feelings in them. Afterwards, they get together in smaller groups and talk about their picture choices.

In the end, all chosen pictures are presented, with the reasons for choosing them, to the whole group. Anyone who prefers to keep their reason to themselves should not be forced to talk, but may simply 'pass' when it is their turn.

Which situations and moods make the group angry? Are there points in common, or are there differences within the group?

35 That Really Makes Me Cross

The group are seated in a circle, and each person is given a sheet of paper on which they are asked to paint situations that make them angry. When everyone has finished, the sheets of paper are placed face-down in the middle of the circle and shuffled. One after the other, the sheets of paper are turned over and the group tries to find out who is made angry by what.

There has to be trust within the group to get involved with each other as openly as this. The aim of the exercise is to learn to understand each other better and to be able, in the future, to prevent aggression-triggering situations for individual people about which others may not have been aware.

Furious Associations

Each person writes the word 'anger' on a piece of paper, and draws a frame around it. Then they write around it all the associations they can think of, regardless of word class; for example:

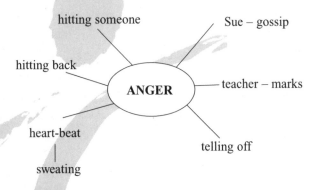

Afterwards, the individual associations are looked at together and – if desired – explained, discussed and compared. The group can also create a large 'anger map' together, using a large piece of paper or a wall poster. The 'anger map' can be put up in the room in which the group meets and added to gradually. Every time someone thinks of another association, for example, something triggered by a group discussion, they write it down on the paper.

The changes to the 'anger map' should be discussed from time to time. Of course, attempts should also be made to break through some of the 'anger chains'.

(37) **Annoyances**

Each group member writes down what annoys them most in a particular situation, or about specific people. Afterwards, they draw a large circle on a piece of paper, into which the 'annoyances' are entered as larger or smaller proportions, depending on their respective importance (as in a pie chart).

The drawings are initially compared and discussed in a smaller group, before being brought into the large group. In this way, the group may learn what makes individuals feel annoyed (and react aggressively), and what annoys everybody and, therefore, needs to be changed urgently. For example:

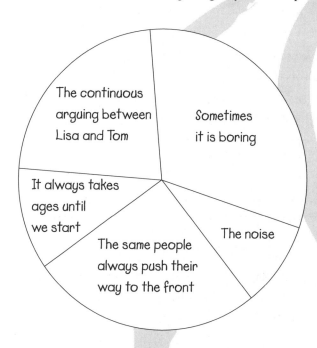

38 What Makes Me Angry

Each person writes down, one under the other, the letters of their first name and, for each letter, tries to find a word that describes events that make them particularly angry. For example:

M maths tests

I idiotic instructions

C chaos

H homework

A all boasting

E envy

L liars

S shouting

A adolescent behaviour

R running for the bus

A arriving late

H having to be home at 10

Afterwards, an opportunity should be given to talk about these individual anger triggers. Maybe there are situations that make everyone in the group angry? These can be uncovered through a joint anger alphabet, such as the following:

A arguing for the sake of it

B bad language

C chaotic people

D daily homework

E egotism

F faking

G grovelling

H having to be home at 10

I idiots

J   jealousy

K   kindergarten behaviour

L   losing

M   miserable people

N   narrow-mindedness

O   obscene remarks

P   phoney people

Q   quibbling over nothing

R   rage

S   stupidity

T   telltales

U   utter stupidity

V   vagueness

W   waiting

Z   zero respect

39 Bag of Anger

The group leader prepares a bag full of small objects (for example, scissors, table tennis ball, matchstick, string, paper, pen, ink, and so on). Each person takes out of the bag the item that they can most easily associate with aggression. Why have they picked a particular item?

40 Angry Sentence Beginnings

The children are given pieces of paper on which are written different beginnings to 'angry' sentences. For example:

When I am angry, I …
My best friend makes me angry when …
My girl friend makes me angry when …
I hate going to school because …
What annoys me most is …
When other people annoy me, I …
I always have to …
My dad says that when others annoy me I should …
When others are annoyed I …
Hitting is allowed when …

Initially, each person completes their sentence for themselves. Afterwards, completed sentences are discussed and compared in small groups. The sentence beginnings should involve the group situation. If there are tensions or actual conflicts, the exercise can serve to reflect and work on these.

41 Bursting With Anger

Each person is given a balloon to blow up. They then imagine a situation that could cause them to 'burst with anger'.

One at a time, the group tries to find out another person's anger trigger. If they guess right, the person in question has to burst their balloon. The game is over when everyone has given vent to their anger. To make sure that no one cheats, it is recommended that the group are asked to write down their imagined 'anger situation'. Group members need to know each other fairly well for this game to succeed.

Better Understanding Oneself & Others

Lack of confidence and fear in social situations, prejudice and the rejection of the unfamiliar can cause and maintain social aggression. Therefore, getting to know each other better, and building up mutual trust are imperative in order to increase self-confidence, and thus stem aggressive behaviour.

The process of getting to know each other often shows up discrepancies between the way people see themselves and how they are regarded by others. For a better understanding, it is important to sort out these discrepancies, and to change and enrich presumptions about each other. Games and exercises

enable people to experience in a less threatening way how they have been perceived up to now, and what may possibly have been putting a strain on social relationships. Social empathy grows, and the group members learn to judge better the effects of their own personality and actions on others.

Getting to know oneself and others better strengthens social trust. As a result, tensions are eased, and outbursts of aggression become less likely.

42 Fine Differences

You can only get to know yourself and others better if you observe carefully. At first sight, many things may look the same – without actually being the same.

Each person chooses an apple from a basket of apples of the same type; looks at it, smells it, and feels it all over. Then the apples are put back in the basket and shared out anew.

Did anyone get back the apple they originally picked? How did they recognise the apple? People who appear very similar will behave differently, too. What previous experiences related to this have the group experienced?

43 A Hand Does Not Have to Hit

Many people, especially children, use their hands mostly for hitting, pinching and pushing. In this exercise, they can experience making contact by using their hands in a friendly way. The group sits in a circle and closes their eyes. A leader gives the instructions:

'You are sitting comfortably, both feet are resting on the floor. Concentrate on your breathing. Feel how it comes and goes, comes and goes, comes and goes ...

'You are breathing out all tension and restlessness. You are becoming calmer and calmer ... You are breathing deeply and more evenly ... You are feeling well in yourself ... Now put your right hand in your left hand, with the back of your right hand in the palm of your left hand. Concentrate on what your right hand feels like in your left hand.

'With your left index finger, gently stroke your right hand: first the thumb, then the index finger, the middle finger, the ring finger, the little finger, and back again across the outside of your hand. Now gently feel your way across the palm of your hand. You can feel the hills and valleys, the grooves and curves of your hand. What do you need this hand for? What sort of things can you do with it when it is as soft and relaxed as it is now?'

At this point the exercise can end, or the hands changed over. The exercise can also be carried out in pairs: 'What can your hand do with the hand of another person? What can it do to make both of you feel good?' Initially, pairs should be made up of people who like each other; only when the exercise has become familiar can pairing be left to chance.

Afterwards, ensure there is an opportunity for discussion. How did the group feel during and after the exercise? What do they normally use their hands for?

With Different Eyes

Everyone sees the world from their own perspective. In order to gain previously hidden insights, and thus develop a better understanding of others, we have to learn, once in a while, to leave our own point of view and take a different viewpoint, or to perceive with all of our senses. To start with, all children the group members move freely around the room. Whenever they want to, they stop, and try to find an unusual viewpoint. They then study at the room, particular items of furniture, other people, by, for example:

◆ Squatting down
◆ Lying on their backs and looking up
◆ Bending down and looking back through their legs
◆ Climbing on a chair and looking down from above
◆ Covering one or both eyes (perception through other senses)
◆ Covering one or both ears; and so on.

Which new experiences did the group have? Did they experience something new about themselves and others? Where would they like to have more experiences? Which experience was the most unusual?

(45) Transformations

Each group member imagines they are an animal. On a piece of paper, they note down the name of the animal, an explanation of why that particular animal suits them, and their actual name. They fold up the piece of paper and, initially, keep it to themselves.

Next, the group agrees on an animal for each person. These animals are then compared with the animal into which each person chose for themselves. Did the group decide on the same animal? Did they, at least, name an animal that is similar? With which people were there differences, and why?

Instead of an animal, the group can also imagine themselves as a plant, a vehicle, a piece of furniture, a musical instrument, and so on.

Experiencing oneself and others through metaphors is generally less stressful than direct feedback. In addition, metaphors contain positive and negative feedback – at the same time.

46 Knowledge of Human Nature

Everyone is given a piece of paper, which has the outline of a human body drawn on it. Each person now draws something into this body outline that they perceive to be particularly characteristic of themselves; for example:

◆ A tongue, if they are particularly quick-witted
◆ Ears, if they are particularly good listeners
◆ A heart, if they are particularly empathetic
◆ Closed eyes, if they tend to daydream
◆ Fists, if they have a tendency to hit out quickly, and so on.

The personalised figures are put up on the wall, and the group tries to find out which one belongs to whom. Who was easy to spot, and who was difficult? Did the group discover new characteristics or abilities in individuals?

47 Dream Image

We all have specific images of ourselves and others. We imagine what we are 'really' like, and what we would like to be like. In order to discover these dream images, the group sits in a circle. One chair is put in the middle. One person – voluntarily – goes and sits on it; another stands behind the chair. The standing person now describes their image of the person sitting in front of him; for example:

> 'You would love to have lived during the Middle Ages. You would be a damsel in a castle with long flowing hair …';

or

> 'If you had a choice you would live in the Wild West. You would have the fastest horse for miles around …'.

The person on the chair is allowed to intervene and make corrections, so that the 'correct' dream image is created. The others in the circle are also allowed to make suggestions.

The exercise becomes less public, and thus less incriminating, if the group splits into pairs and every pair negotiates its vision through dialogue. Afterwards, anyone who likes to can tell the whole group about their experiences. Were there unexpected dream roles? Did the group learn something new about themselves? What sort of feelings did the game trigger?

'Wanted' Posters (Personal Descriptions)

The names of the group members are written individually on pieces of paper. Every person draws a piece of paper; if they choose their own names the paper is exchanged. Now, two or three people get together to create 'wanted posters' for the people whose names they have drawn – as sensational and 'media-effective' as possible. They can even invent gangster names and their particular crimes; for example: *'Numbers Mike – break-ins are his particular speciality'* could be on the wanted poster for someone called Michael who is particularly good – or bad – at long division; or *'Tiger Lily – specialising in jewellery'* could be used for an Elisabeth who loves cats and likes to wear necklaces. And so on.

The finished wanted posters are exhibited. Together, the group tries to guess the identities of the wanted characters. Did the people recognise themselves on their wanted poster? How do they feel with such a description?

(49) Fortune Telling

The group sits in a circle; pens and small blank cards are provided. Together, they collect questions that can only be answered by 'yes' or 'no' and writes them on the cards. For example:

'Do you like eating pudding?'

'Do you like dogs?'

'Have you got a "best" friend?'

'Would you walk up to and talk to a famous person in the street?'

The cards are shuffled and put in the middle of the circle face-down. Everybody takes a turn in drawing a card, and reading the question out loud. However, before someone who has drawn a card answers the question, the person to their left has to predict their answer, in writing and without letting others see. Afterwards, the predicted and actual answers are compared. How well do group members know each other? Were there any special surprises with particular questions or particular people?

50 Guessing Wishes

On pieces of paper, the group answer anonymously one or several questions; for example:

'What would you like for your birthday?'

'What is your favourite music?'

'Which famous person would you most like to meet?'

'What qualities do you look for in your friends?'

The pieces of paper are shuffled, and the group now tries to find out together who has written which answers. So that the task does not become too difficult, large groups should be divided into smaller groups consisting of six to eight people.

In order to assign the wishes appropriately, the group need to get involved in conversations and get to know each other a bit better. Did they find out something new about themselves and others? What, in particular, surprised them?

51 I am Thinking of a Person

This game is also known as 'I spy with my little eye …'. This time, however, it is people rather than objects that have to be guessed. One person thinks of another in the group and says, for example: 'I spy with my little eye someone who likes horse riding, who has dimples when they laugh, who has the courage to stand up to people and tell them their opinion.'

The others try to find out who that person is. The first to guess correctly can think of the next person. Guessing can continue until everybody has guessed the identity of one person. In this case, guessing attempts should be whispered or, even better, written down. The level of difficulty in the game varies according to the statements that are made about a particular person, and how well they are known to the others.

How quickly do the 'thought-of' people realise that it is they who are meant? What do they feel like during this? Would they also have described themselves in that way?

(52) Soul Mates

Without being seen by the others, each group member put a small personal item into a bag. One after the other, the objects are drawn from the bag, again without looking. For each item, the group considers together to which person the item might belong. As often as possible, more than one person should be named. A reason has to be given for each guess. Did the group find out the actual owners? Do those people who were assigned the same item really have something in common? Did they realise that beforehand? How do they feeling now?

53 Four-Corner Games

The corners of the room are numbered from one to four. The leader then suggest four sub-headings for a particular main topic, and assigns one sub-heading to each of the four corners. Each person decides on the sub-heading that applies best to them, walks to the respective corner and, once there, chats with the respective group about their choice. Then new 'corner words' are given and new 'corner groups' are formed. Examples:

We want to talk about our *hobbies*.

Everyone who, in their free time, prefers to play sport, go to corner number one.

Everyone who, in their free time, prefers to listen to or make music, go to corner number two.

Everyone who, in their free time, prefers to watch television, go to corner number three.

Everyone who, in their free time, prefers to socialise with others, go to corner number four.

Or:

Which *school subjects* do you like best?

Those who prefer maths, go to corner number one.

Those who prefer English, go to corner number two.

Those who prefer foreign languages, go to corner number three.

Those who prefer not to do any school work, go to corner number four.

The number of the possible 'corner words' is endless. Depending on the headings given, the group can find out a lot about each other in only a short period of time. What did they not know beforehand? Were there any surprises?

Female–male

The group is seated in a circle. Using random selection, pairs of boys and pairs of girls are put together. A boy pair and a girl pair are called into the middle of the circle at the same time. Each pair then has to carry out activities called out by the leader; for example:

◆ Argue with each other
◆ Be nice to each other
◆ Be cross with each other
◆ Comfort each other
◆ Be scared together.

And so on. The game continues until all pairs have taken part.

Do boys and girls express their feelings differently? What exactly are the differences?

Afterwards, roles are reversed, with the girls now trying to behave as they observed the boys behaving, and vice versa. How did the girls and boys feel during this role reversal?

55 Girls' Stuff – Boys' Stuff – Kids' Stuff

The group divides into boys and girls. Both sub-groups put together two lists: one with girls' games and activities, and one with boys' games and activities. Afterwards, the lists are compared and discussed as a whole group. Results are recorded on two wall posters, which have been created together: one for girls' games and activities and one for boys' games and activities.

Were there differences between the two lists and, if so, what were they? Or did both lists actually contain the same games and activities? Where were there particularly marked differences of opinion between boys and girls? Which specific boys' games and girls' games were left over in the end?

56 Triplets

Often, aggressive confrontations and tension occur repeatedly between the same people. To help them learn to get on better with each other, groups of three are formed. So that everyone can play, there can, of course, also be one or two groups of four. (The instructions are expanded accordingly.) Each group works on the following tasks. They have to name:

Three things that none of the children like; for example:

1 homework

2 unfairness

3 tidying up their rooms

Three things that all of them like; for example:

1 holidays

2 swimming

3 good marks

Something that only one of the children does not like; for example:

Person 1: mental arithmetic

Person 2: visiting relatives

Person 3: spinach

Something that only one of them likes; for example:

Person 1: classical music

Person 2: getting up early

Person 3: helping out in the kitchen

The results of the groups of three are discussed afterwards by the whole group. How difficult was it to find points in common, and differences? Is there something *within the whole group* that really is only liked or not liked by one person? Did the group find out things about others that they did not know before?

(57) Guess the Baby

Every group member brings a photograph of themselves as a baby or toddler. These are collected and put into identical envelopes that are numbered consecutively. Each person remembers their number and writes it on a piece of paper. Everyone now draws one of the numbers (if they draw their own, they put it back and take another), and looks for the corresponding envelope.

Who is hidden behind the baby photo? By which features were people recognised? Can the people themselves still remember their early childhood? How do the memories of the individuals differ? In what circumstances did they grow up?

58 Stereotypes of Violence

Our behaviour is often influenced by stereotyped images. If they are not brought to our consciousness, they will often continue to influence our behaviour despite different information about a particular context. Which stereotypes can the group think of, for example, with regard to the topic 'young people and violence'?

The group divides into small groups who are given the task of coming up with stereotyped images for this topic within the next five minutes. These should be presented as 'sculptures', where every group member assumes a part and everyone 'freezes' in a relevant pose.

One after the other, the groups show their sculptures, and the remaining group members try to guess what scenario is being presented. Afterwards, the actors and actresses give their opinions.

Scenarios can be developed further by the group working together. What might the people who are being portrayed be thinking at the moment? How are they feeling? With which people, and with which situations, can individual group members identify themselves most easily?

In the end, the group can discuss whether all the sculptures had something in common. From that, a new sculpture can be developed, a 'group stereotype image' as it were, that highlights the common aspects related to the topic 'young people and violence' in this group.

Controlling & Reducing Anger & Aggression

Individuals as well as whole groups can, often for seemingly trivial reasons, get into a state of anger and general irritation that they are unable to control. This leads to aggressive explosions that not infrequently bring with them further verbal or physical aggression. Some people are unable to bear tension without immediately reacting to it in an aggressive manner. In order for them to practise positive social behaviour, and acquire the ability to solve conflicts, they must first learn to control their own anger, and experience aggressive impulses against others in a controlled way.

Interactive exercises and games can put people who are emotionally charged into a relaxed state, in which the resolution of problems and the trial of non-aggressive solutions become more possible.

Body-oriented exercises play a special role here because they accommodate the need of young people in particular for movement and, at the same time, demand and facilitate togetherness and mutual consideration.

(59) Rocket Launch

A rocket launch can serve well to release tension. The group enacts the following sequence:

◆ Drumming on the table with their fingers, quietly and slowly at first, then faster and more and more loudly
◆ Hitting the table with their flat hands, or clapping their hands, also with increasing loudness and increasing tempo
◆ Stamping their feet, again quietly and slowly at first, then increasingly faster and louder
◆ Humming and buzzing quietly, increasing to a loud scream
◆ Noise and movement increasing more and more, the group members jumping off their seats, throwing their arms into the air with a loud scream – the rocket has been launched.

Slowly, the group sits down again. Their movements calm down. The noise ebbs away until only a buzzing can be heard that becomes more and more faint until it has stopped altogether – the rocket has disappeared into the clouds.

60 **Shaking Off Anger**

All group members move freely around the room and, at the leader's call, role-play situations in which they have been angry, or situations that made them feel aggressive; how they shook off their anger and rage; and how they then looked forward to something new. This exercise can be used, for example, when members of a group have fallen out with each other. It can be supported with relevant words or music.

The exercise provides people with the opportunity to act out arguments and tension among themselves, through mime and gesture; to literally shake off anger or rage by, for example, shaking their arms and hands, swinging their legs, using their hands to get rid of feelings of fury in their heads, and so on; and then to feel cool and relaxed, smile at each other and meet in friendly encounters, slap each other on the shoulders in a friendly way, nod at each other, or arrange to meet.

61 If I Were Angry

When you feel angry, you do not necessarily have to scream, lash out, kick, or break something. You can also vent your anger in a different way. Everyone has their own anger management strategies. Each group member writes down things that they have done up to now to manage their anger; for example:

- ◆ Ride their bike
- ◆ Hit a punch bag
- ◆ Whistle loudly
- ◆ Run around the block
- ◆ Throw a ball against a wall
- ◆ Have a shower
- ◆ Listen to music
- ◆ Go to bed

The best and most original ideas are written on a poster, and put up somewhere in the room where they are clearly visible.

(62) Swearing Not Allowed

Many people swear uncontrollably when they are angry. In this game, they can practise better self-control. At the beginning, the group decides jointly which specific words are 'forbidden'; or all swear-words which happen to be used by the group are declared to be taboo words. Then everybody takes a turn at telling a story, or questions are asked that tempt the use of 'forbidden' words. Anyone making a mistake and accidentally using a swear-word has to pay a forfeit – for example, sitting backwards on a chair, standing up or kneeling down – until the next person swears by mistake or out of habit.

(**63**) Anger Notes

In one corner of the room, a number of paper 'anger notes' are displayed. They are always available. If someone feels hurt; if they have been teased, and if they cannot or do not want to express their feelings directly, these are there simply as 'first aid' to let off steam.

The anger notes have been prepared together by the whole group; for example, they may have a special jagged shape, a special colour, perhaps dark red or they may carry the heading 'anger notes'.

The angry person takes an anger note, and writes down what it is they are feeling at that moment, using any words that come to mind. Then they screw up the anger note and throw their anger away, for example onto the floor, against the wall, or in a special 'anger bucket'.

From time to time, all the anger that has been collected in this way is destroyed together at a friendship or peace party – unread, of course.

Only initial anger is decreased through use of anger notes; subsequent solutions to problems do not become redundant, but often are only made possible through this process.

(**64**) Anger Doll

Role-play enables people to find out through acting how they can behave when they are angry and annoyed. In doing so, many will find it easier if they do not have to play themselves. With the help of an animal, a play character, or a special 'anger doll', they can express and deal with their feelings and moods, their fears and aggressions more easily. They can make the doll do and say things that they would not admit to themselves.

However, an 'anger doll' can also serve as a substitute for anger: group members can use it to get rid of their built-up anger without verbally or physically hurting those people whom they really have in mind.

Commercially available glove puppets can serve as 'anger dolls', but the group can also make their own from, for example, socks, gloves or similar soft materials that they can always use to carry out 'substitute fights'.

(**65**) Anti-Anger Pictures

Each person initially paints an 'anger picture' on their own, which shows what causes them to become particularly angry, and how they express their anger. In conversation, the group then tries to find constructive forms of management for the painted problems and fears for each person. The solutions are drawn or written on to small coloured pieces of paper, and stuck to the original 'anger picture', so that they stand out. This is then given as a present to the person who has painted the picture, as a visible sign of understanding for their anger, and as support during the management of their aggression.

(66) Friendly Sayings

Everyone knows mean, aggressive, and ultimately stupid phrases that can be used against others. But do they also know friendly, non-provocative, 'stupid' sayings that can be used to counter them? On their own, or in smaller groups, the group members invent friendship sayings. These can be written on posters and put up on the wall or, if written on sheets of paper, can be given as presents, when a person is in particular need of friendship and support. Friendship sayings could, for example, read:

'Always be friendly to strangers.'

'Don't get angry, come and join us.'

67 Trials of Patience

So that everyone can recognise when another person's supply of patience is running out, a length of wool is hung up on the wall for each person. During the group session people can cut or tear off a bit of their thread every time their level of tension rises.

Others can then see at a glance: be careful, his patience has nearly run out, do not provoke him unnecessarily!

68 A Spell Against Anger

After helping the group to settle down and relax, the leader sends them on an imaginary journey:

'Close your eyes and listen into yourself. Somewhere deep down in your body there is anger, well hidden most of the time, but sometimes it comes out suddenly, whether you want it to or not … Feel your anger … Where is it located? … Go through your whole body … What does your anger feel like now? … What is it doing at the moment? Now imagine you could pour all your anger into a magic jug … Carry your anger really carefully, so you don't wake it up … pour it into the jug … be careful that not even a drop of anger gets lost … The jug casts a spell over your anger … When you pour it out again, it has changed … You'll see in a moment … Pour from the jug … What has happened to your anger? … Has it become an animal that quickly runs off? A tree with gnarled branches, that creaks and sighs? A dinosaur that stands up and makes threatening noises? A rock, big and heavy and firmly positioned in the ground? Or …Listen into yourself. Your anger has disappeared. You have put a spell on it. It has been warded off. You are free and calm, really relaxed and satisfied … You have conquered your anger …'

After the imaginary journey, time can also be given to paint the anger in its new form, and to ward it off forever in its new form outside the person.

Without Anger: Keeping Calm

With the help of the following imaginary journey, the group can learn to resort to helpful self-instruction when they feel aggression coming up, or to invent new situations of their own. The leader creates a relaxed atmosphere and then gives the following instruction:

'Today, you are going to visit another planet in your dream aeroplane. You cuddle up in the soft upholstery of your seat, concentrate on the sound of take-off … the humming gets louder and louder … the aeroplane takes off … you are leaving the Earth … already new planets begin to appear … glittering and sparkling … the Earth is left behind … it becomes smaller and smaller … You are feeling light and weightless … you are floating through space … You decide to land on the next planet, you are curious to find out what is there, what you will experience, whether there are people there like you … The closer you get to the planet, the more beautiful it becomes … everything is covered in warm, light, friendly colours. There are houses, round and warm, between them colourful flowers and green shrubs … Everything is calm and friendly. Your aeroplane lands really gently … you get out … you walk across the soft, warm floor … Carefully you walk towards a house … you look through a window … no one notices you … In the house, there is a school class … You can just make out one child saying something to another, but you can't understand the words … It must have been something unpleasant … Or maybe the child addressed just hasn't understood properly what was said? In any case, you see how the child begins to get angry … he is breathing heavily … he clenches his fists … But there, what happens now? … All of a sudden, the child stops. He begins to breathe calmly, in and out, in and out … And he begins to talk, first very quietly, then louder and with more confidence: without anger – calmly, without anger – calmly … And all the time, he becomes calmer and friendlier, and the other child, too, becomes calmer and friendlier … You see how both of them relax … they begin to smile, to talk to each other, they are calm and friendly towards each other … everything is fine …

'No one has seen you at the window … You duck and sneak back to the aeroplane. You tell yourself, "That was a good idea: no anger – keeping calm. I must remember this." You repeat this to yourself several times … again and again … in your thoughts you get back into your aeroplane … you fly back to the Earth … it is becoming bigger and bigger … you are here again … quietly, you say to yourself the words: no anger – keeping calm, no anger – keeping calm …'

After the imaginary journey, there should be an opportunity to think and talk about feelings during and after the journey.

(70) Writing Against Anger

It is difficult to talk with others about feelings of hurt and powerlessness, especially when you are not clear about your own feelings and do not want to admit them. It is easier to write things down. Simply putting into words your own feelings can have a liberating effect. Therefore, the group members should be given an opportunity whenever they need it to write down anything that excites or moves them. For this, a 'writer's corner' could be made available in the group room. If they want people can open their text to the group later, by exhibiting it in a specifically dedicated place. No one should be forced to do this, though. It is also helpful to encourage the group to keep a diary. Joint reading of published diaries and/or joint writing of a 'group diary' – a book is available in the room that can be used by anyone – can serve as an introduction.

Advice on writing letters can be a further support to help group members get closer to their feelings and learn to manage them. Whenever they need to, people can write 'anger letters' (anonymously if they want to). These can be posted into a special 'anger letter box' and answered by an advisor who can also remain anonymous. In any case, letters should be treated with strictest confidence.

Through a letter, intimate details can be revealed, while keeping a distance. A personal answering letter can be read repeatedly by the recipient, and might provide an impetus to have a good look at their own feelings. 'A letter does not blush', as Cicero knew many years ago.

71 Quick Responses

Situations loaded with aggression can sometimes be defused when the 'victims' react surprisingly and quick-wittedly. Unfortunately, often you can never think of something appropriate at the decisive moment. Here, 'quick responses' can provide a remedy.

In response to verbal abuse you could, for example, react as follows:

'You snotty-nosed brat!'	'You're right; have you got a tissue I could have?'
'Weakling!'	'I'm afraid so, yes. You couldn't just give me a hand, could you?'
'Stupid idiot!'	'Be glad I am stupid – otherwise you would be nothing special!'

On their own or in groups, the group can think of unusual responses to aggressive approaches; collect them, and then talk about them as a whole group. The effect can be tried out through role-playing small scenarios.

This may help individuals to remember more original responses rather than simply becoming aggressive themselves.

72 My Anti-Anger Book

Each person will find their own ways of dealing with their anger appropriately. To become more aware of these and to always be able to recall them again and again, the group starts 'books' with tried and tested 'anti-anger methods'. In their books they express, through pictures they have painted themselves; collages; their own or others' writings, and so on, what makes them angry; what other feelings accompany their anger, and what they do or want to do in order to deal with their feelings in such a way that they do not hurt themselves or others.

The first page of each 'book' should be reserved as a page on which to express what the person perceives as positive in themselves and their environment; for example:

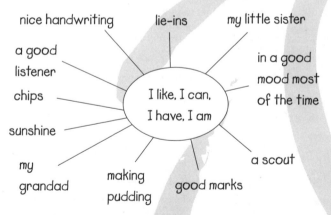

On the last pages, the others in the group tell the individual what they perceive as positive and likeable in them. The books can be used again and again as a memory aid, and should be updated or changed from time to time.

(73) Anger and Rage Protocol

Many people get annoyed easily without really knowing why. And many get angry quickly, although they do not actually want to. Others swallow their anger, or do something unreasonable. In order to get to know themselves better, to learn to deal with anger in a controlled way, an 'anger and rage protocol' which, for a while can be recorded daily, can help. For example:

1 What annoyed me today?

2 How did I react? (Not at all, I cried, I ran away, I screamed, I lashed out, I annoyed someone who was not even involved, I asked for help, waited for an opportunity for revenge, and so on.)

3 How do I want to react next time?

4 I imagine the situation again and practise the reaction that I have written down under 3. (For example, I say loudly in front of the mirror: 'No, I don't want that.' Or I practise breathing deeply and consciously. Or I practise a positive self-instruction. Or …)

The technique of anger and rage protocols should be introduced to the group. This ought to be preceded by discussion and practice of what are helpful reactions to anger, and what are not. The group leader should also take time to discuss anger and rage protocols with the group members individually, to acknowledge them and encourage them to keep going, to introduce changes, and so on.

(74) Writing Angry Letters

Each group member thinks of a person they are cross with; who they have come into conflict with; someone who hurts them or annoys them. In a letter, they tell that person – making things perfectly clear – about everything that they have always wanted to say, but never had the courage to. When everyone has finished with their letters, an opportunity is given to talk together about what sort of feelings they experienced while writing the letters. How are they feeling now they have got things off their chests?

Afterwards, the angry letters can be kept permanently in a safe box to which no one has a key, or they can tear them up into shreds and 'throw their anger to the wind'.

75 Swearing Competition

Small groups are formed to enter into a 'swearing competition' with each other. For five minutes, each group collects (in writing) as many horrible swear-words as possible. Afterwards, the groups read out their abuse to each other, accompanied by corresponding mime.

How did the group feel during the exercise? Did they deliberately choose some words because they wanted to get back at individuals or another group? Do they feel particularly affected by specific swear-words?

Do they actually know all the word meanings? Do they realise what they usually throw at each other in terms of abuse?

(76) **Wrong Number**

Two people at a time talk on the phone to each other. They adopt a typical telephone posture; younger groups can also use a toy telephone, if one is available.

One person picks up the receiver, pretends to dial the other's number and, as soon as they answer, begins to hurl abuse and complaints at them. The person who has been called cannot get a word in edgeways. Finally, one person bangs down the receiver – the game has finished. Afterwards, roles are reversed.

How do the participants feel? Which role is easier to cope with – hurling abuse or to be hurled abuse at? Who terminated the conversation? And why did the abused person listen for a while rather than immediately putting down the phone?

77 The Bad Mood Game

Sometimes a group can have an off-day. On these days, the 'bad mood game' can possibly help, for which each person needs a scarf, a cloth or something similar.

The group members put the scarf or cloth around their shoulders and move around the room. Each person is allowed to take another's scarf off their shoulders – without tearing it! – and throw it onto the floor. The person who has been 'undressed' then grumbles: 'Oh no, my scarf has gone', picks up the scarf, only to throw it onto the floor again and have a good go at the person who took the scarf away from them. Only then do they put the scarf back around their shoulders and join in the game again. It is important that they first vent their own anger before having a go at others. The group should practise not immediately attacking others when they are angry, but, first of all, having a good look at themselves.

(78) Yes or No

The following exercise can help to express underlying or unspoken aggressive feelings. Each person finds themselves a partner who they do not like much, or who 'gets on their nerves'. Both now enter into a dialogue in which one person is allowed to say only 'yes' and the other is allowed to say only 'no'. They stand opposite each other, look each other in the eye, and begin an 'argument'. Pace and volume of speech may be raised up to a level of loud abuse, but all other words remain forbidden right until the end.

After a previously agreed period of time, the exercise is interrupted by a loud signal (for example, a gong or a whistle). Where necessary, a second round, where roles have been reversed, can follow.

How do the group feel after the 'yes–no argument'? Were they able to get rid of some tension? Can they now say a couple of friendly words to each other, or give each other a hug? What was more pleasant: saying 'yes', or saying 'no'?

79 **Putting the Pressure On**

The group form pairs and compare their strengths in a range of tasks. Is it always the same child that is stronger? How do you feel when you are in the weaker position? And if you have the upper hand? What can you do to prevent the feeling or experience of being in a weaker position developing into aggression? What can you do to ensure that those in a superior position do not take advantage of their powers and hurt the other person physically or psychologically?

Possible tasks:

◆ Keeping their bodies rigid, group members try to push each other away – arms and hands stay tightly next to the body, kicking or other use of the legs is not allowed.

◆ The group members position themselves opposite each other, and stretch out their arms so the palms of their hands touch each other. Then they try to throw each other off balance by skilfully pushing the palms of their hands together.

◆ The group members lift their arms, take each other's hands, and clasp fingers. Then they try to push each other away. Arms have to stay lifted throughout.

◆ Pairs of people stand back to back, and try to push each other off their places by moving only their trunks: for example, by pushing, waggling bottoms, and so on. Arms, hands, legs and feet are not allowed to be used here, either.

◆ One person stands behind the other, and puts their arms around the waist of the person in front. The person who is being held tries with all their strength, but without using their hands, to break free (for example, by tensing their muscles and pushing against the other person's hands). After a while, roles are reversed.

(80) Thumb Wrestling

Instead of using the whole body, pressure can also be applied using only the fingers. Even people who are not very strong stand a real chance with this, because winning requires not only physical strength, but also speed, skilfulness and concentration.

Two people stand or sit opposite each other. They stretch out their right or, if they are left-handed, their left arms and lock fingers with each other; only the thumbs retain their free movement.

The winner is the person who manages to hold down the thumb of the other with their own thumb.

81 Arm Wrestling

For this exercise, two people of roughly equal size sit facing each other across a table. Both put their right (or their left) elbows on to the table and clasp hands. Their free hands are kept behind their backs. At the leader's command, each person tries with all their strength to push the lower arm of the other on to the table.

The same exercise can also be carried out lying down. The participants lie facing each other, rest one elbow on the floor; clasp hands, and try to push the lower arm of the other to the floor.

This exercise should be carried out on carpet, or outside on the grass or in sand, to make sure that no one gets hurt.

82 Cockfight

Two people at a time stand facing each other. They cross their arms in front of their chests, lift one leg so they are only standing on one, and then try to push each other off balance by knocking arms together. While doing so, they are not allowed to uncross their arms.

The aim is to remain standing for as long as possible, and not to have to put the second foot back on the floor.

(83) Fight of the Crabs

Two people at a time become 'crabs'. This means that they are allowed to move forward using only their hands and feet; arms, legs and stomachs are not allowed to touch the floor. Then each person lifts their right foot and tries to push the other 'crab' off balance, so they touch the floor with their right foot – or even their whole body.

Pulling, pushing, jerking and similar hand or body movements are allowed, but definitely no hitting.

84 Mirror Fencing

Two or more people at a time stand facing each other and carry out a 'pretend fight' with each other. One person begins with an appropriate 'fighting' movement, the other(s) respond(s) with a 'counter' movement. Talking is not allowed during the fight, and no actual touching is allowed to take place.

The fight is called off after a set period of time.

(85) Power and Powerlessness

The group forms pairs. They take it in turns to be powerful or powerless; for example, slave-driver and slave; angry dog owner and small dog; strict teacher and scared pupil; dominant and dependent couple, and so on. The 'powerless' person has to do everything that the 'powerful' person commands them to do. However, that person must not ask for anything impossible *and must, under no circumstances, hurt* the 'powerless' person. Certain basic fairness rules ought to be discussed beforehand. Any breaking of those rules will lead to an immediate stopping of the game. After a little while, roles are reversed. Finally, an opportunity for discussion is given.

In what ways do power and powerlessness feel different? How much does one feel at the other person's mercy when one is in the 'powerless' position? Or is there anything one might be able to do to make the best of a difficult situation?

86 Back-to-Back Duel

The group forms pairs. Each thinks of a swear-word, or something else unfriendly that they have always wanted to say to the other person. They then write it on a stiff piece of paper and have the piece of paper attached to their backs.

Now the pairs begin the 'back-to-back duel': each person tries to look at the back of the other to decipher the unfriendly message. At the same time, they have to try not to let the other person see their own back.

Before the duel begins, the holds and movements that are permitted, and those that will lead to the duel being stopped are discussed.

Did everyone manage to find out their respective partners' criticism of them?

87 Putting One's Foot in It

Two people at a time stand facing each other, and hold each other by the hand. Between them, a piece of newspaper lies on the floor which could, for example, be a pretend cow pat. Each person now tries to pull the other over so that they are forced to put their foot in the cow pat.

88 Spoon Fencing

The group members split up into pairs. Each person is given two spoons, one for each hand. One spoon remains empty, while an eraser, a ping pong ball, or anything similar that comes to hand, is put on the other.

Now the pairs begin fencing with their empty spoons. They are only allowed to touch spoons, not each other. The winner is the person who manages not to spill the object from their other spoon for the longest time.

89 Book Ends

The group members split up into pairs. Each pair is given a rolled-up newspaper, or a similar paper roll. The pairs position themselves away from each other, so that they can just about touch each other with stretched out arms plus paper rolls.

A thick book is placed upright in front of each person's feet. Now the 'fight' begins. The fighters have to try to 'hit' each other with their paper roll. They may only aim at or below the neck – faces are out of bounds. The loser is the one whose book falls over first.

Western Duel

Two people at a time carry out 'Wild West' duels. Only four movements – two movements with their counter-movements – are allowed. These are agreed and practised prior to the start of the actual duel, because, during the game, for each movement the corresponding counter-movement always has to be made. For example:

◆ If one person pretends to draw a gun, the other has to raise both arms.
◆ If one person pretends to draw two guns, the other has not only to raise their arms, but also to close their eyes tightly.

Both people are not allowed to 'shoot' at the same time; this means that they have to watch each other carefully, and wait for the 'right' moment. If there is a mistake – that is, if both do 'shoot' at the same time – or a wrong counter-movement is made, both are defeated.

91 You are Coming with Me Now

The group members stand in twos in two loose rows opposite each other. First, the people from one row try to pull their counterparts from the other row around the room, against their passive resistance. While this is going on, they are allowed to engage in a simple dialogue, such as the following:

'You are coming with me now!'
'No, I don't want to!'
'But I want you to come with me now!'
'Get lost!'
'But you have to!'

And so on.

After a few minutes, roles are reversed. Now the other person pulls.

Power and resistance should be applied and experimented with in a playful way. The group finds out what happens when there is a little bit of giving in; what happens when there is no giving in, which consequences simultaneous verbal pressurising can have, and so on.

The aim of this exercise is to get to know one's own feelings and strengths when pulling and resisting.

92) Letting Out Air

Lots of balloons are handed out in the group. Everyone blows up a balloon and tries to make it burst by sitting on it. The game can also be played as a 'chain reaction' game: the first person blows up a balloon; the second person sits on it, blows up another balloon for the third person, and so on.

Relays are also possible: which group will be 'deflated' first?

(93) Balloon Fight

Each person is given a balloon, on which they draw angry faces and attach them to short sticks. Using this 'balloon brute', the group now carries out 'pretend' fights, either two people at a time against each other, or in a general free-for-all.

The fight must only be carried out with the balloons, not with the attached sticks!

94   Back to Back

This game not only enables young people to get rid of surplus energy, but, in particular, it enables those who do not think that they have much strength to experience how strong they actually can be in a group situation.

The group forms two rows and everyone links arms. The two rows then turn and stand back to back. Each row tries to push the other away. At the same time, the rows must not be pulled apart.

The game can be played by varying the line-ups of the rows. Is it a good idea to place smaller or weaker people in the middle of the row, or at the end? Does it make sense to alternate weak and strong people? What does it feel like to be a 'strong' or a 'weak' link? Can the game help supposedly 'weak' group members to feel strong opposite 'strong' people? Can it facilitate solidarity within the group?

95 Having a Go at the Audience

The group members form two smaller groups. A leader makes sure that previously agreed rules are adhered to. Each group prepares by collecting accusations, insults and swear-words to be used against the other group. Perhaps a conflict situation can be suggested, to which the accusations should relate. (5 minutes)

The groups sit or stand opposite each other, with some 'safety distance' between them. At a signal (the groups having decided beforehand who is going to start), one group begins to swear as loudly and angrily as possible at the other group: the whole group has to be addressed; *personal insults are not allowed*. The other group is not allowed to fight back, but has to simply let everything wash over them. At a second signal, swearing must stop immediately. (1 minute)

The groups reverse roles. Now the previously sworn-at group is allowed to swear. (1 minute)

The groups hurl abuse at each other simultaneously. (1 minute)

Finally, the members of both groups walk towards each other and hug each other. (1 minute)

Afterwards, there has to be an opportunity to talk about the feelings that came up during the game. How much hostility and anger were people actually capable of in an artificial situation? How difficult was it to let the abuse wash over yourself, without being able to fight back immediately? Do you dare to say worse things when you are with others than when you are on your own? Does the hug in the end 'make everything all right' immediately? Ritualised swearing can have a relaxing effect when there is an underlying tension or conflict within the group: for example, it can cut short a tedious, unsatisfying discussion. Afterwards, a real conflict resolution often becomes easier.

96 Paper War

For this exercise, old newspapers or magazines are needed. The group divides into two equally large sub-groups. The sub-groups each mark out a 'battlefield'. The 'battlefields' should be of equal size. When a whistle is blown, everyone begins to make paper balls from the newspaper and throw them at the other group. The group who, after the whistle has been blown again, has the fewest balls in their field, can be declared the winner.

It is just as much fun when everybody plays against everybody else. The paper war finishes after a set period of time. Together, the group can then make a big 'peace ball' from all the small paper balls. The 'paper war' can be played in many variations – for example:

◆ Players are only allowed to throw balls while they are sitting or kneeling
◆ They have to use their feet instead of their hands to throw the balls
◆ They are only allowed to throw over their backs, or behind them through their legs
◆ Everyone has to throw with their left hand (left-handers with their right hand).

97 Soccer

For each person who wants to play, at least one sock is required, which is worn instead of shoes. Using chalk, a playing field is marked off. Items of furniture have to be moved out of reach. A carpet in a group room, a mat in the gym, or a sandy or grassy area in the playground are ideal for this game.

Each person now has to try to remove another's sock, and to transport it out of the playing field, keeping their own sock on for as long as possible. Anyone who has lost their sock has to leave the playing field. Players can put their sock on again outside the playing field, and throw themselves back into the crowd.

Of course, the game can also be played with two socks per person. So that no one can get hurt, the group of 'sockers' should not be too big. The game can be practised with just two people. The bigger the crowd becomes, the more fun there is. For safety reasons, groups should not be bigger than 10 to 12 people. It is important that adherence to the game's rules is monitored: only pulling off socks is allowed; kicking, pinching and so on are not. *As a precaution, glasses should be taken off before the start of the game.*

(98) Survival Training

The whole group kneels on an 'island', which has been marked out using chalk or tape, and support themselves by putting both hands on the floor. They then have to try to push each other off the island, without taking their knees or hands off the ground. The game can be finished after a set period of time, or it can end when there is only one person left on the island.

99 Together Against the Baddies

For this game, a certain amount of space is needed, such as the carpet area in a group room, the gym, or a patch of grass in the playground. Two people – the 'baddies' – stand in diagonally opposite corners; the rest of the group stands between them. The 'baddies' want to bring the others under their power, but can only do this when they are together and holding hands. That is why the children have to try to prevent them getting together. They are allowed to stand in the way of the 'baddies', but are not allowed to hold them, trip them up, and so on. Rules are agreed together prior to the start of the game; a violation of the rules leads to the game being stopped.

This game enables young people to appreciate that they can be strong together against attacks, and that superiority requires not only physical strength, but at least as much attention, skilfulness and solidarity.

(100) Wagging Tails

Each person imagines they are an animal. They tuck a handkerchief or a piece of tape loosely in their waist band or belt. Accompanied by a lot of animal noise, each person now tries to get hold of as many 'tails' as possible. They are only allowed to use their hands to grab tails – not to hold other children, and so on.

As a variation of the game, a large animal can be built from all the small animals. Every person who has lost their tail holds on to the person who has taken it. In this way, lines of varying length are created. All tails that have been taken are put in the waist band or belt of the last person, and the game continues. In the end, will there be only one large, strong animal left?

This game enables people to get rid of aggressive impulses in a ritualised way and, at the same time, facilitates the development of a sense of community.

(101) Stake

If tension has built up between two people in a group or between the group and leader, relief can be provided by 'repentance' at the stake. One or more people stand in the middle at an imaginary stake. The remaining group members form a circle around them. At a signal, they begin to dance around the stake and demonstrate all their anger with threatening gestures and war chants. Only touching of the prisoner(s) is strictly forbidden. After a few minutes, roles are reversed. The people at the stake are relieved. No one must be forced to take part, or talked into participating in the game.

However, everyone who wants to vent their anger at those standing at the stake also has to take a turn standing at the stake: anyone wants to experience power must also experience for themselves the feelings of the powerlessness.

Building Up Inner Strength & Self-Esteem

Socially aggressive young people often appear to be strong and self-assured but, in fact, inside they are unsure of themselves, and dependent on the opinion of others. Powerlessness arising from weakness is a cause of many – often seemingly incomprehensible – aggressive outbursts.

Positive self-esteem reduces uncertainty and fear, and thus the tendency to act aggressively. A self-confident person is able to perceive and respect their own as well as others' limitations. They can communicate their needs and wants; they have learned to voice and to take criticism without developing feelings of helplessness, fear and guilt that could then possibly lead to an outburst of aggression. People who lack self-esteem are often no longer able even to make positive comments to others, never mind being able to accept positive comments, because they are unable to integrate this with their own negative self-image. They presume that other people perceive them in exactly the same way as they do themselves. That is why people with low self-esteem tend to misinterpret harmless comments and behaviours of others. As a result, attempts by others to make contact often fail.

Enabling young people to experience themselves as valuable, and to develop self-esteem gently through play is, therefore, an important step in reducing socially aggressive behaviour. Self-esteem and inner strength are requirements for the positive development of human skills, entering social relationships and taking responsibility for one's own actions.

(102) I Am – I Can – I Have

Cards are fixed to the group members' backs using sticky tape. Each card has the phrases 'I am …', 'I can …' and 'I have …' written on it, one under the other. Now everyone takes a pen and begins walking around the room. As they do so, they complete each other's sentence beginnings with positive comments that are really appropriate for the individual concerned. The game ends when all sentence beginnings have been completed.

Everyone now removes their cards and reads what the others think of them. The writers remain anonymous. This may give someone the courage to tell another something they may not dare to say. How did they feel while they were walking about? How are they feeling now they have read their cards? Are they surprised about the comments, or do they have a similar opinion of themselves?

(103) Who am I?

Each person is given 10 small pieces of paper on which they write 10 different, brief answers to the question: 'Who am I?'

Anything can be written down that comes spontaneously to mind: first name; age; sex; different roles, such as child, sister, brother or pupil; favourite activities, favourite meals or drinks; special abilities; particular weaknesses; wishes or fears. Once all the pieces of paper have been written on, each person sorts them according to their significance: the most important item for their self-portrayal is put first; what is least important is put last.

Afterwards, the whole personal hierarchy is compared and discussed with the others in the group. Did the group mostly write down external characteristics? Or did they have a good look at the person inside themselves? Did they learn something new about themselves?

104 The Person in the Well

The group are seated in a circle. One person stands in the middle. All of a sudden, the person in the middle collapses and complains: 'I've fallen into the well!' The remaining person ask in unison: 'Who should rescue you?' The person in the well answers, for example:

'The person who can scream loudest', or
'The person who can comfort best', or
'The person who has the bluest eyes'; and so on.

When a particular requirement has been named, everyone in the circle tries to meet that requirement as convincingly as possible. The person in the well decides, on their own or with the help of the group, who best fulfils the named criteria. That person then 'rescues' the person in the well by reaching out their hand and helping them up. Afterwards, they become the next person in the well.

The leader should make sure that it is always different person who is allowed to rescue the person in the well. The game can also be used to portray emotions. The person in the well then names only emotions that the others have to portray through mime; for example:

'The funniest person', or
'The angriest person', or
'The saddest person'; and so on.

During this game, the group members can experience the fact that they all can do something particularly well, and can all help someone else.

105 The Same and Not the Same

No person is 'better' or 'worse' than the others; and, despite all their differences, everyone also has something in common with the other group members. Everyone is worth something. In order to recognise this, the group members have to be given an opportunity for appropriate experiences.

The group should be seated in such a way that each person can see everyone else. One after the other, they are given instructions such as the following:

Stand up and touch, one after the other, everyone who
is wearing a red item of clothing.
Touch everyone wearing sandals.
Touch everyone wearing a watch.
Touch everyone who is a boy or a girl like you.
Touch everyone with the same hair colour as you.

If the exercise is carried out more often, the group themselves will begin to think of more things that everyone has in common, or that are unique. Maybe they will also discover that those people they do not like are, in many ways, just like themselves.

(106) Higher – Bigger – Further

Once in a while, every young person needs the feeling of being the 'biggest'. The following competition can help to achieve this. The group rewards or claps for the 'best' or the 'only', related to given criteria or abilities. For example:

Who is the tallest child?
Who can stretch out their tongue the furthest?
Who can build the highest tower from matchboxes?
Who can learn by heart the most telephone numbers in three minutes? And many more.

Of course, the leader has to make sure during the selection of the questions that indeed every person wins once, and that the selection criteria of the group are perceived as something positive by the group.

Afterwards, a discussion can bring out the fact that every person is special, and that there are many more outstanding abilities or characteristics than we are generally aware of.

(107) Hot Chair

The group is seated in a circle. In the middle stands the 'hot chair'. Here, the person who currently is most in need of positive attention takes a seat. They then move the chair around the circle, stopping at each person in turn. Each person tells them something that they like about them: for example, their good ideas; the way they care for their little sister; their beautiful handwriting, or their fashionable hair cut. Afterwards, the group can talk about how you feel when you have to say something nice to someone you do not actually like very much. And how do you manage to accept so many friendly comments in public?

Everyone should get an opportunity to sit on the 'hot chair'.

(108) I am Proud

Often, we only remember the bad experiences. However, everyone will also have learned or experienced something positive recently that they can be proud of.

The group members are seated in a circle and, one after the other, complete the sentence beginning: 'I am proud that I …'; for example:

… had the courage to walk past a big dog all on my own.

… did not lash out and hit Peter when he annoyed me.

… have learned to jump off the three-metre board.

No one should be forced to contribute. The group leader too may tell what they are proud of. How difficult is it to remember something positive? How do you feel when you talk openly about it? What did the group like particularly about what people said? What might they also be able to try?

109 Chocolate Side

The group members are seated in a circle. Everyone is given a piece of paper and a pen. After a little reflection, they write down three adjectives which, in their opinion, describe their three best characteristics – for example: funny, clever, helpful; fast, honest, sporty. They should try to change their handwriting a little, for example by writing in capital letters, so they are not easily identified. Pieces of paper that have been written on are folded up and well shuffled before they are put in the middle of the circle. One after the other, each person takes a piece of paper (if they pick their own this should quickly be exchanged for another), reads out the adjectives, and tries to recognise the corresponding person, providing reasons for their decision. If they have guessed wrongly, the others are allowed to help.

What does it feel like when you are only allowed to say positive things about yourself? And how do you feel if that is then read out aloud and rationalised in front of the group? Does the positive self-image that a person has differ from the way the group perceives them?

110 That's What I am Like

In order to develop identity and self-esteem, young people have to consciously look at themselves. They can do this by, for example, writing the word 'Me' in large letters on to a piece of paper, and trying to present their personality using form, colour and decoration.

111 On the One Hand and on the Other Hand

Everyone has both good and bad characteristics; and sometimes behaves well and at others behave not so well. In order to be able to cope with these contrasts, and maybe even change them, you must first of all get to know them. Everyone is given a pen and paper, and completes the following statements:

This is what I can do particularly well – these are my good characteristics:
This is what I can't do so well – these are my poor characteristics:
This is what I like about myself:
This is what I do not really like about myself:

Afterwards, the descriptions are compared. The group will find out that they each have something that they like and something that they do not like about themselves. Do they want to remain like this? Do they want to change something? Can they help each other? Can they do something together?

Throwing Out Ballast

Hold a group discussion about what rights each group member has, and put together a list. For example, each person in the group has the right:

- ◆ To be treated with respect
- ◆ To be listened to
- ◆ To their own opinion
- ◆ To their own feelings
- ◆ To be unique
- ◆ To make mistakes
- ◆ Not to be bossed around
- ◆ To be in a bad mood
- ◆ To join in games
- ◆ To determine group activities.

Now ask everyone to imagine that they are floating on their own in the basket of a hot air balloon. On board, they have 10 bags containing the above rights. All of a sudden, the balloon begins to lose height. To delay the descent, ballast must be thrown out. Each person must throw out the bag with the right that they think they can most easily do without, then the second least important one, and so on, until only one bag containing one of the rights is left. The balloon will now remain in the air at the correct height until it has reached its destination.

Essentially, each person has the task of putting the 10 rights from the group's joint list into a personal hierarchy. Afterwards, discuss how individuals made their decision and why.

How difficult did each person find it to make the decisions? How big are the differences between the group member? From this, what implications are there for group members to get on with each other? What implications are there for the way individuals must be treated?

(113) Dark Clouds – Clear Sky

When a person is angry, this can be like a gale or thunderstorm, like dark clouds or sharp points. When a person is balanced, this can be like blue sky, sunshine, a beautiful flower, round shapes, or gentle colours. Each person divides a piece of paper in two, each half representing a feeling. On one side, the group members draw their anger, their fury, their tears and their desperation; on the other, they draw their joy, their calmness, their balanced nature and their feelings of harmony. Afterwards, the whole group looks at the pictures and talks about them.

If the pictures are hung up in the room, they provide visible evidence for all that each person – even someone who becomes angry quickly, and has an 'aggressive' reputation, also has harmonious and friendly feelings, and that everyone who appears to be gentle and nice, also has aggressive and nasty feelings. In corresponding situations, a look at the pictures can help to avoid increasing someone's aggressive behaviour through negative comments and counter-aggression.

114 Seeing the Positive

Positive thinking is the magic key for the development of self-esteem, and therefore also offers the key to acting constructively, and in a socially acceptable way in difficult situations.

Each group is likely to have certain members who are known to be 'aggressive'. People who 'act aggressively' have often learned early on in their lives that they 'are aggressive' and that that is something bad. They will be able to behave differently if they can gain a positive self-image, and experience that 'being aggressive' is initially something positive. It can mean 'to be forceful' and makes a statement about a person's inner drive.

Each of the so-called 'aggressive' people selects a small group for themselves. Together, they then compile a list in which the person's aggression is assessed positively. For example:

> I am good because I say what I feel.
> I am good because I am active.
> I am good because I have strength.
> I am good because I tackle things.
> I am good because I say clearly what it is I want.

For each person, at least three positive interpretations have to be found. Afterwards, the group thinks of ways in which the strength and energy of that person can be applied positively during arguments or other pressurised situations.

Was it difficult to interpret 'aggressive behaviour' positively? Which experiences did the so-called 'aggressive' people have during this exercise?

(115) Own Names

Some people's names have meanings. They may recall particularly important events on the day of their birth – for example, a beautiful sunrise – or they express the hopes that the parents have for the child. Names of Native Americans can relate to particular achievements of a child, or characterise their personality, such as 'Clever Fox' or 'Gentle Feather', and can be changed during the course of a person's life.

Which names would the group give themselves? Ask each person to think on their own, or in a small group, of a fitting name that belongs to them alone. How did they come up with their new name? How do they feel with it? Which name would they prefer to be called by the group in the future: the name they have chosen for themselves, or their 'official' name?

116 Better than Running the Gauntlet

The group members stand facing each other in two lines, and make a passage. One at a time, they then run from one end of the passage to the other. But instead of running the gauntlet, and being teased and annoyed, they are smiled at and touched in a friendly way. If they stop in front of someone – for example in front of someone they do not get on with that well – that person must look them in the eye and say something really nice; for example:

> I am your friend.
> Something I like about you is that you are always in a good mood.
> I think it is brilliant how you can work things out in your head without using a calculator.
> Do you fancy playing with me during break?

And so on. If someone is lost for words, they can simply give the person who is 'running the gauntlet' a big hug.

The exercise can also be used as a feedback exercise, or as a special 'present' for birthday children, to greet people after a long absence', as a farewell, and so on.

How do the group members feel in the different roles? How difficult is it having unexpectedly to say something nice to someone?

Building Non-Aggressive Relationships

Despite a strong need for social acceptance, many young people in particular fail again and again in their attempts to make contact with others. First they have to learn to adapt to others and, in the meantime, hold back their own needs. They have to get rid of fears of contact and tolerate closeness. When they have rid themselves of physical taboos, they will be able to enjoy non-aggressive physical contact.

Children and teenagers must agree to play *with* each other, rather than *against* each other. They need to experience how much security and pleasure they can gain when they do something together with, or for, others. During games and exercises where they have to adapt to the movements of others, they experience common ground and the need for teamwork.

The development of non-aggressive relationships creates positive feelings for each other, and provides the foundation for constructive conflict resolution.

(117) Standing Up – Sitting Down

The group members walk through the room, swinging their arms and legs; they walk – according to the leader's instruction – quickly or slowly. Next, the group form pairs and walk together. Gradually, they synchronise their movements. Without talking to each other, they move in harmony. Without a word, one person takes the lead, and the other copies. The roles can be changed several times – still without a word.

At a signal, the pairs form groups of four. They find chairs and sit in a small circle. They are still not allowed to talk; eye contact is the only form of communication allowed. One person at a time stands up and sits down again. At any one time, only one person is allowed to move; arrangements take place without words, until finally everyone remains seated quietly.

Was it difficult not being allowed to speak; to be led or to lead without any words? Were there people who tended to take over the leader's role more readily? Were there others who tended to be led?

(118) Body Buildings

The children form groups of six to eight. At the command of the leader; they carry out given tasks using their bodies. For example:

Build a robot!
Build a vehicle that can move through the room!
Build an animal that can chase off others!
Build a house that can protect!

Of course, any relevant noises must can be made. The exercise can be varied by changing the constitution of the groups, while keeping the task the same.

Which group could fulfil the task best? From these playful body sculptures, could there be consequences in the case of an emergency? For example, could the group members work together to protect each other in threatening situations?

(119) Shelter

Three to five children get together. One is declared the master builder, and joins the others together as a 'hut' into which the 'master builder' enters and makes himself at home. Afterwards, roles are reversed, so that each child gets an opportunity to build their own protective hut.

What does a hut need in order for you to feel secure in it? How do the children who are giving the protection feel? How do those being protected feel?

(120) Talking Hands

Two children sit facing each other. They close their eyes and try to hold a conversation using their hands. Did they actually succeed? What did they talk about? What did they feel like while they were talking? How often were they tempted to resort to using their voices and to open their eyes?

The exercise becomes easier when a topic is agreed at the beginning, which then has to be discussed using the hands. The children could be given the task of working on a particular topic first in an excited and angry manner, and then in a friendly and harmonious manner.

(121) Teamwork

The group form pairs and are linked by two thin wooden sticks, approximately 30cm long, which must not have sharpened ends. Alternatively, new, unsharpened pencils could be used. The sticks are held between fingertips or the palms of the person's hands, using only a little pressure. The pairs now have to solve small tasks without dropping or breaking the sticks. During this activity, they are not allowed to talk. Possible tasks could be standing up and sitting down together, climbing over an obstacle, tying a bow, and so on.

The exercise can be made considerably more difficult by increasing the size of the group to three or four people.

How unfamiliar was the teamwork? Which tasks were easier, which more difficult to master? Which techniques for 'sticking together' were developed? How difficult was it to communicate without speech?

(122) Where all Rage Ends

In a group discussion, everyone describes a place where they do not feel angry; where they do not have to be aggressive; where they feel comfortable; where they can be calm, satisfied and totally relaxed. They imagine how and what they would be feeling there: on their skin; on their tongues and teeth; on their hands and feet; arms and legs; in their hearts and stomachs, and so on. They imagine what they would hear and see, smell and taste if they were at that place.

Then they close their eyes and try to relax and to picture, just for themselves, a place where all anger has ended. Afterwards, the group talks about what each individual person, and the group as a whole, can do to change the real place where they all happen to be together, so that it becomes more like the places where all anger ended.

Back Communication

The group stand or sit one behind the other, so that each person can comfortably reach the back of the person in front of them with their hands.

The last person in the line draws a 'secret message' – a sign, number, letter or something similar – on to a piece of paper, and then puts the piece of paper somewhere where it cannot be seen by anyone else. The person at the other end of the line is also given a pen and paper.

Then the last person in the line begins to 'draw' their message on to the back of the person sitting in front of them. Using their hands, that person passes on the message on to the next back, and so on until everyone has received the message. The last person draws the message they have received on to their piece of paper.

Afterwards, the piece of paper with the original message is compared with the final message. How much of the original message is still recognisable? How did the group feel during the 'back transport'? Did it feel uncomfortable to have someone 'on their back', without knowing what they were going to do?

124 Getting Close

The group practise closeness and togetherness by getting together as closely as they can; that is, they try together to take up as little space as possible.

To do this, it is best for them to start off with a larger space, which is marked out on the floor with chalk or tape, and then move closer and closer together. The game can be played several times over a number of days. The increasing closeness can then be demonstrated through the shrinking of the marked-out base.

Initially, the spatial distance between the participants can also correspond to the actual emotional distance between them. The space occupied illustrates how close – or distant – they are to each other.

(125) Gordian Knot

The group form smaller groups of 12 to 15 people. The members of each group now position themselves in a fairly tight circle; stretch both arms towards the middle of the circle; close their eyes, and give each other their hands blindly.

On opening their eyes again they check – making corrections where necessary – that they have not taken the hands of the person standing directly next to them, and also that they are not holding both hands of the same child. If all is well, the Gordian knot is ready.

With a little patient teamwork, the knot can now be undone, without letting go of hands, so that everyone ends up holding hands in a circle. Did they manage it? How did they feel during this Gordian knot?

(126) Stroking Hedgehogs

Not everyone directs their anger and fury outwards. Some people become more and more reserved: they put up an 'all-round defence', and make it difficult for themselves and others to take up positive relationships.

The group divides into pairs. Initially, one person turns into a 'hedgehog', puts up 'all-round defences' by rolling up tightly (drawing up their knees, closing their eyes, with head on their knees, and arms wrapped around the knees), and tries to imagine that they feel hurt and offended. The other person tries to get them out of their state of isolation. They can stroke the 'hedgehog'; talk to it; gently roll it back and forth, and so on. Of course, they are not allowed to break up the defences by force. Often, it helps to imagine what they themselves would find persuasive in such a situation. Afterwards, roles are reversed. At the end, the opportunity is given to talk within the group about what experiences the children have had while putting up 'all-round defences', and while 'stroking hedgehogs'. By what means was tension relieved most effectively? What caused new tension? Did everyone feel similarly, or were there personal resistance and very personal methods of relief?

'Stroking hedgehogs' is a very intimate game. *That is why no child must be forced into joining in.*

(127) Joint Fury – Joint Peace

The group splits into small groups of two to four members. Each small group is given a large piece of paper that is divided into two halves by a line. Together, they begin by drawing an 'anger' picture in one half, and then they draw a 'harmony' picture in the other half. When everyone has finished, the pictures of all the groups are exchanged and discussed by the whole group.

What sort of emotions did the participants experience during their joint drawing of anger? What sort of emotions did they experience during their joint drawing of peace and harmony? Did they actually draw 'jointly' at all? Did some group members push to the front while others tended to keep back?

(128) Group Picture

Each person is given a large piece of paper. Now a topic is given, and everyone begins to draw a picture to fit the topic. After a short time, at a signal, they pass on their piece of paper to the person sitting on their left. That person adds further detail to the picture, until the instruction to pass on the pieces of paper is given again.

What do the pictures look like when all the pieces of paper have gone around the group once and are back with the original artist? Did they really try to work on the topic and let a 'group picture' come into being? How difficult was this?

Would it make sense to add another round, in order to 'complete' the pictures?

(129) Window Techniques

The group divides into small groups of three to six; each person is given a different coloured pen. Each small group sits around a very large piece of paper, which has been divided by a cross into four equally sized 'windows'. A picture is now drawn into each window:

◆ *Top left:* Each group member draws anything that they can think of, fencing their drawing off.

◆ *Top right:* Everyone tries to fill the space with their picture, disputing each other's right to the space, drawing over the pictures of the others.

◆ *Bottom left:* Everyone takes turns to draw, trying to add to the shared picture.

◆ *Bottom right:* Giving time and attention to each other, everyone draws simultaneously a picture that is as harmonious as possible.

How did the group experience the different 'window techniques'? Which one was the easiest? Which one was the most unpleasant?

130 Anti-Rage Airman

Apologising or joining in activities after a temper tantrum is difficult. Many people quickly calm themselves down again, but can only hesitantly communicate this with words.

For such cases it can be helpful to have some 'anti-anger planes' available. The paper planes are made during a calm moment, and then labelled with the most common 'peace messages'. For example:

I am sorry!
Can I join in your game?
I would like to work with you.
I won't annoy you again.

And so on.

The 'anti-anger planes' are always ready and waiting for deployment in one corner of the room. If they are needed, each person can use them without having to say a word, and send a 'peace message' to another person or to the group.

(131) We Belong Together

The group try to link up their forenames into a kind of crossword puzzle. The starting name is always that of someone who is to be highlighted; for example, because it is their birthday; because they are new to the group, or simply to tell them that they belong to the group, and so on.

	S	T	E	P	H	A	N	I	E
	A								
U	R	S	U	L	A			T	
	A				L	I	L	O	
	H		S	U	E			N	
					X			Y	
					A				
	D	O	M	I	N	I	C		
					D				
					E				
		I	N	G	R	I	D		

(132) Feeling Good Within the Group

Anonymously and with disguised writing (capital letters are best), everyone writes down what they are frightened of in the group; what makes them feel threatened, and what makes them feel angry. The pieces of paper are collected in a box and then attached to wall posters, so that no piece of paper can be traced back to a particular person, and no one needs to be frightened of sanctions.

One after the other, the fears and threats thus collected are discussed and topicalised in the group, so that, in the course of time, everyone in the group can feel safe and happy.

Instead of using words, fears can also be expressed through picture drawings. How frightened are individual people of revealing themselves? Do their feelings change over the course of time? Does the atmosphere within the group change?

(133) Friendship Magic

Everyone is allowed to put a spell on three other people so that, in the future, they will be friendly and nice towards them. Using a 'magic wand' – for example a ruler – the individual taps the three people on the shoulder one after the other, and says a magic spell. For example:

'Michael, I am turning you into a boy who doesn't push me when I walk past him.'

'Anna, I am turning you into a girl who doesn't make fun of me when I can't do something.'

'Andrew, I am turning you into a neighbour who doesn't constantly claim my half of the table for himself.'

The enchanted group members have to listen quietly to the spell and think about its message. They are not forced to keep the spell – but maybe they will change a little.

What did the group members feel during this game? What did those who were casting spells feel like? What about those members who were enchanted?

It is a relief not to have to respond to the criticism, and not to be put under pressure to change. This can create a favourable situation for perhaps secretly taking the spell to heart.

(134) Secret Friendship

For an agreed period of time (one to two days for younger people, several days, a week or a month for older ones), each person turns another with whom they often argue, or do not really like, into a secret friend. During this time, they pay particular attention to positive behaviours of this person. Older people could write down their observations as a 'friendship report', where they record concrete events and observations. The 'secret friendship' also requires the group members to support their secret friends discreetly, through words and deeds – for example, choosing them for the next turn; voting them into their group; supporting their wishes and arguments during a group discussion, and so on.

Once the agreed period of time is up, the group can talk about their experiences with the secret friendships. During this discussion, secret friendships can be revealed if desired. What sort of experiences did the group have? Did any secret friendships actually turn into open friendships?

Giving Presents

The group members write their names on pieces of paper. The pieces of paper are shuffled. Each person takes a name. Then they think of a really personal present for that person, write it down and add their own name as sender. For example:

For Billy: 'I am going to help you with your homework today.' Mary

For Robert: 'I am going to choose you for my team at the next football game.' Ali

For Holly: 'I am going to lend you my scissors until you have got a pair of your own.' Mike

'Giving presents' is a good way of ending a group session. The 'presents' are read out aloud, and the group members thank each other. Of course, all presents that have been announced have to materialise.

Such presents also lend themselves to reconciliation after a fight, or to relaxation after a particularly exhausting period of working. They can replace the usual Christmas presents, or be given to individuals on special occasions: for their birthday; to speed recovery after illness; or for better settling into a group, and so on.

How do the people who are giving the presents feel? How do the people who have been given presents feel? How difficult is it sometimes to find a suitable present?

Resolving Conflicts Peacefully

Conflicts are created when different interests and needs clash. Many people, especially adults, experience conflicts as threatening, and thus try to avoid them where possible, or 'turn them off' quickly. Therefore, it comes as no surprise that young people often feel helpless in the presence of conflicts, or resort to aggressive forms of conflict management: they have never learned to do anything else. Generally, they have learned that the 'stronger person asserts themselves', and that they have to 'defend themselves'. However, aggressive confrontations and threatening behaviours do not solve conflicts. They remain alive under the surface, and weigh down relationships again and again.

Life without conflict is impossible. That is why the question is not so much how to avoid conflicts as how to cope with them fairly and appropriately. Conflicts do not have to escalate into power struggles and fights, but, instead, can be seen as an opportunity for clarifying points of view, and for improving relationships.

True conflict resolution requires that people learn to respect each other, and to state and assert their rightful interests without hurting themselves or others in the process. Interactive exercises and games not only reduce the number of conflicts within a group, they can also contribute to dealing with conflicts more consciously and without aggression, and to developing new, creative ideas for their resolution.

A trusting, relaxed group atmosphere, mutual trust and the common aim of working towards a conflict solution that can be subscribed to by everyone, are requirements for non-aggressive conflict resolution.

(136) When Two People Have an Argument

The group divides into sub-groups of three. Two people begin an argument about any topic – for example, something that frequently leads to arguments within the group – with the second person continually contradicting the first, even if that means that they have to argue against their personal views. The third person has to try to 'settle' the conflict with additional arguments. Of course, they will not be able to do this in the short amount of time available, as those arguing are not allowed to change their point of view.

After about five minutes, roles are changed around so that each person in turn has the opportunity to take on each role.

Afterwards, the whole group discusses their experiences, and thinks about what is required in order to really settle the argument. Perhaps the group can jointly come up with some 'argument rules'?

137 Scissors, paper, stone – the Japanese Way

Playing scissors, paper, stone to decide a question just uses the hands – the Japanese version uses the whole body.

The symbols are as follows:
◆ *The Samurai*: a large step forward and stab with an imaginary sword
◆ *The lion*: threatening gestures with both hands shaped into paws with claws, accompanied by dangerous growling
◆ *The little Japanese mother*: hunched back and shaking hands.

The game works as follows: the Samurai kills the lion with the sword; the lion eats the little Japanese mother; the little Japanese mother, however, has power over the Samurai: out of deep respect, he refrains from killing her; his sword remains by his side.

After explaining the figures and the power relationships, the group can play against each other individually or in two groups. During a group game, each group chooses together which figures they will be – at the leader's signal or after a count of three – portrayed by each child.

Playing scissors, paper, stone the Japanese way is particularly suitable for getting rid of emotional tension, because it does not require a lot of moving around, but, during group games in particular, the portrayals are likely to cause laughter.

(138) Sitting Out Anger

Conflicts should be resolved by those people who are involved in them. A good way of doing this is 'sitting out' conflicts on special 'anger chairs'.

The two people arguing sit opposite each other in a corner of the room, and throw any accusations they want to get rid of at each other – the only thing that they are not allowed to do is become violent. Only when the conflict has been resolved are they allowed to participate in the group's activities again. For younger groups, it is a good idea to mark the 'anger chairs' accordingly, for example with angry faces and flaming colours, and to reserve them for the sole usage of sitting out arguments.

In addition, anyone who simply feels angry can withdraw to an 'anger chair'; and must not be addressed until they reintegrate themselves into the group.

The Child who Conquered Anger

The leader begins to tell a fairy tale about 'the child who conquered anger'. The story can be invented, or may take up a true event from the group and turn it into a fairy tale. After the first three or four sentences, the children take it in turns to continue the story. The task is to find or invent jointly an outcome where the anger is conquered.

A discussion during a break in the story or afterwards can settle whether the group really succeeded in finding a solution. Then the story can be told once again from the beginning (or from a break in the storytelling), with a different story line and ending.

The different solutions can exist with equal validity, or the group can agree on a solution that everyone is happy with.

Argument Games

The group members get together two at a time and role-play a given argument that frequently occurs within the group. For example:

◆ One person owns some coloured pens; another person always uses them for their own drawings without asking and, on top of that, breaks them.
◆ One person is standing right at the front of a queue (during lunch, when getting on the bus and so on), then the other person comes along and jumps the queue.

The participants discuss the problem, with one taking on the role of the disturbed or affected person, and the other taking on the role of the disturbing or attacking person. After a little while, roles are reversed. If possible, the group or the pairs should try to find a solution for the conflict. The solutions are then presented within the whole group and discussed.

Mediating Arguments

The group imagines that two of them – let us call them Peter and Paul – have been friends for many years. They are almost always together and, most of the time, they get on well. Of course, they do argue sometimes. However, one day, they are really angry with each other. They never want to see each other again. Why are they so angry with each other? And what could be done to make up again? It would be so silly if this long-term friendship was to break up because of a single argument.

Initially, each person tries on their own to find answers to these questions. Afterwards, they present their solutions to the group and consider together which might be the best, which they have successfully tried themselves, or want to try when an argument next occurs.

(142) Changing Perspectives

The group sit in a circle. In the middle, two people, who have a conflict to resolve, sit opposite each other. Each is asked to put themselves in the other's shoes, and to present the conflict from the other's perspective.

The two people should then try to find a common conflict solution, while at the same time continuing to represent the position of the other person. The remaining group members are allowed to intervene constructively when the conversation slows down, or if the two 'forget themselves'.

Which feelings are the conflicting pair moved by? Is it possible to find a satisfying conflict resolution?

(143) Three Wishes

The group divides into groups of three. First, each person writes down three special wishes related to a given topic. Then, the small groups discuss these wishes and agree on one for their group. The chosen wishes are then discussed in the whole group by everyone until they have agreed on a single wish. Wish topics could be, for example:

◆ Where would you most like to go on holiday?
◆ Which game would you most like to play next?
◆ What would you most like to have for lunch?

What sort of experiences have the group had? Was it difficult to come to an agreement? Who was able to push through their own wish? How did they do it? Did everyone actually try to push through their own wishes, or did some people give in right from the start?

(144) Shipwrecked

In a shipwreck, the group manage to save themselves by getting into a small boat with which they can reach an uninhabited island, as long as the boat is not too heavy. Apart from the clothes that each person is wearing, a total of only 10 items can be taken on board, otherwise the lifeboat will sink. Items have to be selected according to their importance for the group's survival on the island.

First, each person puts together their personal list of 10 items they need for survival. Next, small groups (three to five people) are formed who have to come up with a common list of 10 items taken from their individual lists. Once this is done, each small group sends a representative to take part in the 'council of shipwrecked people', who then have to come to a final decision with regard to the 10 items.

For this purpose, the 'council' meets in public: the people belonging to the council sit in the middle and negotiate loudly. Everyone else sits in a circle around them and observes the negotiations.

How did the final list come about? Was it easy to reach an agreement, or were there conflicts? What sort of conflicts? How did the negotiations in the (non-public) small groups, and in the (public) council group proceed? Did each person always feel well represented? Can each person accept the final decision, even though they initially wanted to take something else?

(145) Pros and Cons

A pros and cons discussion takes place to deal with a particular dispute. The participants form two groups, one of which collects pro-arguments and the other contra-arguments – regardless of the individual opinions in the dispute. The pro- and contra-arguments are contrasted, for example by writing them on two wall posters, and then discussed. At the end of the discussion, the two opposing points of view can be summarised and presented by one member from each group. Then the group votes. Which arguments are more convincing? What are individuals voting for? Is there a tendency within the group to decide on one or the other 'side'? Is it actually necessary to make a decision at all? Are there some disputes that cannot be solved through discussion? Is it possible for opposing arguments and points of view to exist next to each other, without people having to argue about them? Can we simply accept that others may have different opinions from our own?

Unresolved Conflicts

Everyone can bring to mind unresolved disputes. Feelings of anger and powerlessness that have not been dealt with influence every new conflict. In order to cope better with these feelings, it is necessary to have a good look at the frustrating experience, rather than trying to 'pull oneself together' or 'suppress' it.

To do this, everyone sits comfortably and relaxes. They close their eyes and breathe calmly and evenly. The leader then addresses them as follows:

Think of a fight or argument that made you feel both angry and helpless at the same time, and that still occupies your mind. Now try to go beyond 'thinking about it' and relive the fight or argument. Put yourself back in that situation. Where were you? What did you do? What did others do? How did you feel? What did you hear, see, smell, taste? What were you wearing? Did you say anything? What did you say? What did others say? Remember once more every single word, experience every gesture, every movement, every feeling …

Were you able to really put yourself back into the conflict once more? Now let the memory go again. Let it be. If it has annoyed you, relax again. Pay attention to your breathing. Breathe calmly and evenly, calmly and evenly …

Now experience the same event again more. This time, however, you are not yourself, but the other person who made you so angry. Imagine you are that person. You have their thoughts, their movements, their feelings. What is it like being that person? How are you experiencing the incident now?

Were you able to experience everything once again? Now slowly shake off the memory again …

When you are ready, become yourself again and slowly come back to the room, to the group, to the here and now.

How did the group feel during this exercise? Could they really relive that previous situation? Could they really feel themselves into the role of the other person? What are they feeling now? Can they understand themselves and the other person better now? How do they feel now when they think about the conflict of that time? Have anger and powerlessness changed? How would they act now in the conflict?

(147) Old Burdens

Real disputes from at least a day ago – so that anger and aggression have already subsided and a conversation is actually possible – are portrayed through role-play by those who were originally involved, or by other group members.

The group then tries to find out together what the argument was actually all about, and whether and how it could have been prevented; whether it could have been carried out more constructively, or what could have been done instead.

If such 'old arguments' are recur afterwards on a frequent basis, some ground rules should be noted down which can then help to manage future problem situations without, or at least with less, aggression.

(148) Council of Elders

The leader tells the group the story of two estranged Native American nations who, together, have to build a bridge to get to their hunting grounds. One nation owns the forest that could provide the wood, the other has the necessary tools.

The group now divide into two, representing the two estranged nations. First, each 'nation' lists the problems that prevent the two working together. Then they enter negotiations through their 'elders' (two or three people from each group). The elders keep checking back with their people, and so develop new suggestions for solutions, until a final common solution has been found.

When this process has been perfected, it can, of course, also be used to deal with actual conflicts within the group.

149 Conflict Report

A clear head and an ability to stay calm are needed for solving conflicts. That is why, before every conflict resolution, taking a deep breath is recommended ; also counting up to 10 (or 20 or 100 – depending on how agitated a person is); running around the block once, and so on, and viewing the conflict as objectively as possible with the 'inner eye', and putting together, in writing, a conflict report, which provides answers to the following questions:

Who did I argue with?
What did I want to achieve?
What did the other person try to achieve?
What did I say and/or do?
What did the other person say and/or do?
How am I feeling now?
How might the other person be feeling now?
What could I do to bring the argument to an end?
What could the other person do in order to finish the argument?

With the help of the report, those involved in the conflict should initially try to find a solution. Only when they are unable to do so should the group or the group leader be approached for support.

How difficult is it to analyse a conflict situation that one is involved in as 'objectively' as possible? Are there particular conflict themes that occur again and again? Are there people who I always end up arguing with? Why might that be the case? What could I do about it?

(150) Legal Advice

Arguing people or groups elect a 'solicitor' for support. Of course, these people are not allowed to be involved in the conflict themselves, but, instead, have to try to represent the opposing points of view of their clients as objectively as possible, and to find a way of sorting things out.

During the conflict negotiations, those involved are only allowed to take the floor when specifically asked to do so by their solicitor. From time to time, the solicitors can interrupt the negotiations to consult their 'clients', and to come up with new settlement offers.

The conflict solution is deferred, and continues to be negotiated until an appropriate solution that can be accepted by both parties has been found. All arguments must stop for the length of the negotiations; the 'clients' have to behave neutrally.

How difficult was it to let an argument 'rest'? How difficult is, not being allowed to interfere with the conflict resolution, but instead having to leave the negotiation to the solicitor? How much of a relief can it be, too, not having to negotiate oneself?

(151) Matters of Dispute

In many groups there are conflicts that always flare up again and again. By uncovering such disputes, conflicts can be prevented, and possible conflict solutions can be practised.

On a wall poster or a large piece of paper, which is laid out on the floor, the group collect 'their' matters of dispute and causes for conflicts. For example:

> The other gang always hangs out at our meeting point.
> Our teacher is unfair.
> My best friend always plays with someone else.
> Daniel always pushes in front.
> I always have to go in goal when we play football.

The group discusses which conflicts occur most often, and how they have been resolved up to now. Is everyone satisfied with the present action, or could there possibly be better solutions? Could it even be possible to prevent the conflicts occurring in the first place, or at least nip them in the bud at the earliest opportunity?

Are there matters of dispute that are connected, possibly along the following lines: if this happens first, then that is going to happen afterwards; or when I have an argument with my friend, don't I often have an argument with my mum afterwards?

The most common and most important matters of dispute are shared out among small groups. They have to come up with possible solutions that are presented to the whole group, for example through role-play, afterwards.

Are the suggestions realistic? Are there still other possibilities? Which ones could we try out the next time we have an argument?

Peace Offerings

Conflicts often happen because the wishes and needs of children are not met, or because adults fear negative consequences. These potential conflicts can be defused by the children's 'peace offerings'. To come up with such peace offerings for predictable – and presumably recurring – conflicts, the following grid (with examples of conflicts) can work well:

My wishes	*Possible conflicts*	*My peace offering*
To see a particular film on television.	'You are always sitting in front of the television.'	Record the film on video, agree a 'convenient' viewing time with my parents.
Cycling to school on my bike.	'That is far too dangerous.'	Pass a road safety course first.
Sit next to a particular child at school.	'You'll just be talking all the time.'	Agree a 'behaviour contract' with my teacher.

The completion of such a grid can be done as partner or small-group work. First, those wishes that always seem to lead to conflicts can be collected by the whole group.

Afterwards, the 'peace offerings' are discussed. Which one did actually help? Which undertaking was easier, which more difficult, to keep?

The exercise becomes particularly effective when the adults involved also come up with 'peace offerings'.